Vegetarian
STUDENT
Cook Book

SILVANA FRANCO

MEREHURST

Published in 1995 by Merehurst Limited
Ferry House, 51–57 Lacy Road, Putney, London SW15 1PR

Reprinted 1996

Copyright © 1995 Merehurst Limited

ISBN 1–85391–459–2

A catalogue record for this book is available from the
British Library

Series Editor: Valerie Barrett
Design: Clive Dorman
Illustrations: Keith Sparrow

Typeset by Clive Dorman & Co.
Colour Separation by P&W Graphics Pty Ltd, Singapore
Printed and bound in Great Britain by
Mackays of Chatham PLC, Chatham, Kent

RECIPE NOTES

35 Indicates dishes that cook in under 35 minutes

- Follow one set of measurements only, do not mix metric and imperial
- All spoon measures are level
- Always taste and adjust seasonings to suit your own preferences

CONTENTS

INTRODUCTION

For most young people making the move from the family home to college accommodation or the infamous student flat is a difficult step, but if you have the added complication of being a non-meat eater, looking after youself properly, particularly eating well, can be a minefield. Not only is cooking something for you to think more carefully about, but eating out and knowing what to choose when out shopping can turn into a very confusing business. To help you on your way, turn to the Ingredients section on page 12, for an insight into what to look out for when cruising the aisles.

It is very easy for the young veggie to live on cheese and eggs which although may ensure an adequate intake of protein will lead to weight gain, high cholesterol levels, and the lack of other essential vitamins and minerals. You need a balanced, healthy diet to function to the best of your ability both physically and mentally and not only is cooking your own food from scratch the cheapest and healthiest option, it also means you can be sure of exactly what you are eating. It's also great fun. Hold dinner parties and impress your friends with your inventiveness and creativity, and don't forget, if you're living in a shared house full of students, as the cook, you get to skip the washing up.

This is a basic book, with dishes that you will be able to master even if you've never boiled an egg before. All the recipes are very straightforward, giving plenty of scope for you to adapt them and make them your own. Save time in the kitchen by being well prepared and planning what you're going to cook in advance. If your cupboard is well stocked, you should be able to knock up a meal for two without necessarily having to go out for extra ingredients. Most of the recipes in this book serve 2. If you're only cooking for yourself it's still worth making the full quantity and then reheating it the next day or taking it to college with you for your lunch.

A good time-saving way to balance your meals is to cook all-in-one complete meals based on a carbohydrate such as pasta or rice. To help you stick to these guidelines this book includes chapters based upon the four main carbohydrates. If you make dishes that need an accompaniment, steam some fresh vegetables or make a quick salad rather than choosing chips. See page 6 for nutritional information which includes more details on meal planning. Happy cooking!!

For more information and detailed advice about vegetarianism, write to:

The Vegetarian Society
Parkdale
Dunham Road
Altringham
Cheshire
WA14 4QG

EATING WELL

Eating well is the key to getting the best from life and if you follow a varied and balanced vegetarian diet you will feel fit, healthy and full of energy. As with all students, if you plan to cram your revision or study late into the night, it is essential that you eat a well-balanced diet that will not only keep your mind and body fuelled, but can also help prevent heart disease, tooth decay and obesity as well as many other common illnesses. Studies have shown, for example, that you're less likely to get a cold if you have a good intake of vitamin C, which is something to think about if you've got exams looming.

Generally speaking, the more varied your diet the more likely it is that all the vital nutrients you need are being provided. In order to ensure you are getting enough you must be eating from each of the three main food groups detailed below. Having discovered how to plan good balanced meals, you should also take a look at the things you snack on between meals. Try to drink plenty of water and eat yogurts or fruit if you get hungry between meals – sugary drinks and fried salty snacks will just help you to pile on the pounds and offer very little by way of nutrients.

GROUP 1

CARBOHYDRATES

Starchy foods like potatoes and bread are good sources of fibre, vitamins and minerals. Carbohydrates like these should be the base of every meal, they are naturally low in fat, (and as a nation, we consume far more fat than we need), and will satisfy your hunger.

Your body needs carbohydrates to convert into energy but are there are two main types: starch and sugar. When you eat a sugar-filled food or drink, you get an almost instant energy surge, which is quickly followed by a low. Your brain tells you that you need more energy and you crave for another bar of chocolate or can of fizzy pop. Yo-yoing energy levels can leave you feeling lethargic and unable to concentrate on your studies but because starches are digested by the body far more slowly than sugars, they give a constant slow-releasing source of energy which is exactly what you need if you're going into a 3-hour exam. If you have a heavy day ahead, you must eat a proper breakfast. When you wake up, your sugar levels are low so boost

them up with sustaining food. Have a couple of slices of toast and Marmite and a big bowl of muesli or porridge, avoid stimulants such as tea or coffee and have a glass of fresh orange juice instead.

At meal times go for filled baked potatoes, risottos and stews and pair stir-fries, soups or salads with a carbohydrate for a healthy, well-balanced meal. Good carbohydrates include:

rice and grains

pulses: lentils and beans

breakfast cereals: muesli, porridge and Shredded Wheat, not sugar coated Frosties or Ricicles

bread: wholemeal is best but white is still good

pasta

potatoes

noodles

GROUP 2

PROTEIN

The body needs protein for the production of body tissue, so to keep strong and healthy it must be included in your diet. Most people in this country easily consume enough protein but as the highest quality protein comes from animal sources, as a vegetarian, it is something that you must take into consideration when planning your meals. You don't need to consume a lot of protein but should make an effort to include a small amount with each meal. Unfortunately a lot of high protein food is also high fat, so you must also be aware of how much cheese, cream and butter you eat.

The type and quality of protein varies greatly from food to food. Animal proteins such as fish, milk and poultry are the most complete, but there are plenty of good, but not quite as complex plant sources of protein to be found in carbohydrates like grains, pulses, beans and potatoes. The best way to ensure quality, not just quantity is to try and combine proteins so they complement each other, this is even more important for vegans who don't eat dairy produce. Try and eat at least two different foods together to obtain a high quality protein, fortunately this is the way that most foods go together anyway – a good example is beans on toast which is a very good high fibre, high protein, low-fat snack meal. Quality protein foods include:

milk	seeds
yogurt	peanut butter
cheese	seaweed
eggs	grains
butter	cereals
tofu	beans
nuts	pasta

GROUP 3

FRUIT & VEGETABLES

The World Health Organisation recommends that we eat at least 400g, that's almost a pound, or five portions of fruit and vegetables a day – that doesn't include potatoes but does include beans, nuts and seeds. Fruit and vegetables are packed with different vitamins and minerals, so you should try and vary the types you eat and remember that it's impossible to eat too much. Choose fresh or dried fruit in preference to a bar of chocolate or crisps.

The way that you cook the vegetables is of the utmost importance, as it is very easy to destroy the nutrients. Leafy greens are packed with water-soluble vitamin C, so the traditional method of boiling them in water means that when you eat the vegetables you may still get the fibre, but the nutrients and most of the flavour have gone down the drain. Instead try stir-frying, steaming or cooking methods which involve eating the liquid that the vegetables have been cooked in such as soups, stews and pasta sauces.

As soon as they are harvested, fruit and green vegetables begin to deteriorate nutritionally, so don't store them for weeks, eat within a few days of buying. Frozen and canned vegetables are just as good, and in some cases better than fresh. Take frozen spinach for example, it is picked, prepared and quickly frozen within hours, locking in a good percentage of the nutrients

TOP TIPS FOR EATING WELL

- Base your meals on starchy carbohydrates to get a constant supply of energy.

- Ensure you have an adequate intake of protein.

- Cut back on sugary snacks – don't satisfy your hunger with empty calories that leave you craving more.

- Try to avoid stimulants such as chocolate, cola and coffee – keep your mind and body on an even keel.

- Ensure you get enough high quality protein but don't base your diet on dairy produce – eat plenty of nuts and pulses.

- Try and combine your proteins – eat at least 2 together.

- Keep an eye on your fat intake, including butter, cream and cheese.

- Try to eat five portions of fruit and vegetables each day – take care when preparing and cooking vegetables, don't destroy their vitamin content.

INGREDIENTS

Shopping

Although some things are obviously not suitable for vegetarians, there are lots of ingredients used in ready-made things like biscuits and cakes that strict vegetarians need to look out for. Some ingredients such as the E numbers listed on labels are too detailed to go into here. However there is book published by Penguin entitled 'E for Additives' that lists the origins of all E numbers, a few of which are not suitable for vegetarians. Here is a rough guide to help you avoid the pitfalls of shopping.

Gelatine

Made from the hooves, hides and bones of animals it often appears in sweets, jellies, cakes and mousses. It is also used to coat certain vitamin and health capsules such as evening primrose oil.

Animal Fats

Lard and suet are often used in biscuits, pastry and cakes. Animal fats often appear on food labels as E471, however E471 also comes from vegetable sources, so it's hard to be sure exactly where it originated. It is probably safest to try and avoid it where possible. If you discover it in your favourite brand of biscuits and don't want to give them up, you can always write to the manufacturer and ask them if it is animal or vegetable fat.

Eggs

Very few products contain free range eggs. If the item contains eggs, they will have been laid by battery hens unless clearly labelled otherwise.

Cheese

Most hard cheeses have been set with rennet which comes from the stomach of a calf. There are many cheeses around such as Cheddar and Parmesan that have been manufactured specially for vegetarians and lots of cheeses are naturally suitable, but unless they are labelled as so, it is difficult to tell. If you buy the cheese from a deli counter, the assistant should be able to help. Most soft cheeses are naturally suitable for vegetarians as they have not been set hard, and therefore would not have had rennet added – there is no hard and fast rule but generally it is safe to eat: soft cheese, cream cheese, curd cheese, mascarpone, ricotta, brie, mozzarella and feta cheese.

Worcestershire Sauce

Most brands of Worcestershire sauce contain anchovies, so check the label before buying.

Wine and Real Ale

Lots of wine and real ales are filtered through isinglass which comes from fish. Although, there is no fish in the actual drink, some vegetarians do not wish to drink it. Some supermarkets now stock clearly labelled vegetarian wines, and generally organic wines are also suitable. If you want to know, try buying your wine from a wine shop where the information available is more specialised.

FOOD STORAGE

If you've only got half a cupboard and a shelf in the fridge to store your provisions, then you're going to have to think carefully about what you buy, or you'll end up with a cupboard packed with pickled gherkins, 3 varieties of mango chutney, a tub of gláce cherries and no room for your bread or pasta.

Here's a list of all the things you ought to have in store. Apart from the items listed, buy vegetables and salad ingredients to accompany meals, and keep some fresh fruit handy to munch after supper or if you're feeling peckish.

CUPBOARD

ESSENTIALS
- packet of pasta
- packet of long grain rice
- can of chopped plum tomatoes
- can of baked beans
- small bottle of olive oil
- small bottle of vegetable oil
- bottle of soy sauce
- small bag of lentils
- small tub of dried parsley
- small tub of dried basil
- carton of curry powder
- packet of stock cubes
- tube of tomato purée
- bottle of vinegar
- small packet of flour

- bag of sugar
- salt and pepper

NOT ESSENTIAL, BUT VERY HANDY
- jar of English mustard
- bottle of vegetarian Worcestershire sauce
- can of chick-peas
- bottle of tomato ketchup
- jar of honey
- jar of pesto sauce
- cumin seeds
- dried chillies

FRIDGE

There are very few chilled items that are real essentials, but there are some that you will use almost everyday. I have not included fresh herbs, as they are something of a luxury for most students, but why not have a go at growing your own – a small pot from the supermarket is not too pricey and with a bit of attention, will survive happily on a sunny window-sill. Alternatively, if you have freezer space, keep a packet of fresh parsley in there, and simply crumble a handful into your cooking as you need it. Other good things to keep in your fridge are a jar of mayonnaise and a jar of curry paste.

ESSENTIALS
- Milk
- Butter or Margarine
- Eggs
- Cheese (Cheddar and Parmesan). Cheese adds flavour to your cooking so it's well worth shelling

out a little extra for a tangy, mature Cheddar that will really zip up your food rather than opting for the cheaper but blander, mild Cheddars. The same applies to fresh Parmesan. It is expensive, but a little of it, freshly grated, goes a long way. If you're planning to eat plenty of delicious pasta dishes, then the dried, ready-grated variety won't do your cooking any favours as it tends to be lacking in flavour compared to the fresh variety.

FOOD SAFETY

The most important thing to remember when you're responsible for feeding yourself, is to keep the kitchen clean. It isn't all that difficult to give yourself (or your house-mates) food poisoning, but if you cook your food carefully and observe basic hygiene and storage rules, you won't put anybody's health at risk.

Here's a few pointers that you should keep in mind:

- Keep the kitchen floor clean, don't encourage mice, rats and other vermin to set up home in your house.

- Don't let dirty pots pile up, bacteria will multiply at an astonishing rate, making your kitchen unsafe and smelly. While you're cooking, try and wash-up as you go and finish off washing the rest straight after you've eaten.

- Wash up in very hot , soapy water. Use rubber gloves and a scrubbing bush and take care to rinse the dishes well with clean hot water.

- Leave the washing-up to air-dry on the draining board – dirty tea-towels will just spread germs onto a clean plate, so make sure they're laundered regularly.

- Clean up splashes and spillages immediately after they occur as they make the floor dangerously slippery and can become ingrained and harbour bacteria.

- Wash your hands before you start cooking.

- Keep the fridge clean. It's easy to forget a small lump of cheese that's left to go green at the back of the shelf if the fridge is not cleaned out regularly. Mould quickly spreads from bad food to healthy like the one bad apple in the sack. It's not only risky but costly.

- Never keep food past its use-by date.

- If a chilled item has been left out of the fridge and has become warm, play safe and throw it away, especially if it's of dairy origin.

- Store dry goods in a cool dark place. Keep bags sealed up with tape and check sell-by dates.

- Take chilled or frozen food home as quickly as possible and store at the correct temperature. Don't refreeze food that has defrosted.

- Don't reheat food more than once, especially rice dishes.

EQUIPMENT

Whether you choose to lodge in college accommodation or a shared house or flat, more likely than not, you'll have to share kitchen facilities with a group of other students. This can be a bit of a mixed bag of tricks. No doubt you will argue about whose turn it is to wash-up or empty the bin, but on the plus side, you will also have the opportunity to pool resources, and not just borrowing the ketchup from your house-mate's cupboard but sharing kitchen utensils and equipment. Every High Street has a cheap kitchen shop that's an Aladdin's Cave of useful gadgets from spatulas and can openers to salad spinners and fancy vegetable slicers so you should be able to get your hands on the essentials listed below. And don't forget that any piece of equipment you buy is an investment that you'll probably end up using for years.

ESSENTIALS
- can opener
- cheese grater
- rolling pin
- slotted spoon
- fish slice
- potato masher
- pastry brush
- 2 chopping boards
- 3 wooden spoons
- metal hand whisk
- metal sieve
- frying pan
- 3 sizes of saucepan with lids
- 2 sizes of bowl
- 1 large sharp knife
- 1 small sharp knife
- set of kitchen scales
- baking sheet
- roasting tin
- casserole dish with lid

NOT ESSENTIAL BUT VERY HANDY
- garlic press
- vegetable peeler
- measuring jug
- wok

BREAD AND FLOUR

There's nothing in the world more appetising than the smell of freshly baking bread. When you walk into a supermarket that has an in-store bakery, you will always catch the smell of the bread. I'm not sure if they plan it purposefully as the bakery always seems to be at the other side of the shop, but it certainly sets your tummy rumbling and your hand reaching out for a currant bun.

INTRODUCTION

As a student, you probably wouldn't consider making your own loaves of bread, as although it can be very worthwhile, the time and effort involved is a major drawback. Fortunately the range of breads now readily available is quite incredible, from Italian olive breads to Greek pittas and Irish soda bread, it now comes in all shapes, sizes, textures and flavours. So even if it's not freshly baked by your own fair hand, there's no reason why bread shouldn't be a fundamental part of your diet.

STORING BREAD

If you buy your bread fresh from a bakery, it is best eaten the day you purchase it but it will last a couple of days if you store it in a cool, dry cupboard in its paper wrapper to allow the bread to breathe. If it goes hard the next day, pop into a hot oven for 5 minutes to heat through and soften. If you buy sliced, plastic wrapped bread, you can store it for longer because of the additives used in large scale bread production, but it will go mouldy rather than hard after a few days. If you can't eat a whole loaf within a week, keep it in the freezer and pull out slices as you need them.

FLOUR

Even if you're not a baker, you should always make sure you have a small packet of plain flour in your cupboard.

Use it to thicken soups and sauces, coat vegetables for frying, to roll out ready-made pastry, make dumplings (page 26) and batters for pancakes (page 30) and Veggies in the Hole (page 32). If you can remember learning to make puff pastry at school, you will be able to appreciate why ready-made pastry is such a blessing. It can be bought both fresh and frozen and is very easy to use. You will only need to use half a packet to make enough for two, and the remainder can be kept covered in the fridge for a couple of days.

BASIC PIZZA DOUGH

EASY!

Makes 4 individual pizzas
400g (14 oz) plain flour
2 teaspoons, easy-blend dried yeast
1 teaspoon salt
2 tablespoons olive oil
250 ml (8 fl oz) warm water

1 Place the flour, yeast and salt in a large bowl. Make a well in the centre and pour in the water. Using your hand to mix, bring the ingredients together to form a soft, pliable dough. Turn the dough out onto a lightly floured work surface and knead vigorously for at least 5 minutes until the dough is smooth and stretchy. Because all flours are slightly different, you may find that you need to add extra flour or water to get a good, soft but not too sticky dough.

2 Rub a little oil over the surface of the ball of dough, cover with a clean tea towel and leave in a warm place for about 30 minutes until doubled in size. Divide the dough into four equal balls and knead them again for a couple of minutes. Roll out the dough to the size and thickness you like, remembering that it will be at least double in thickness by the time it is cooked, and place on baking sheets.

3 Preheat the oven to 240C,475F, Gas 9. By the time the oven has heated up, (about 15-20 minutes) the dough will be ready for cooking. Arrange the toppings on your pizzas, except the cheese, if using, and place in the oven for 10 minutes. Sprinkle over the cheese and return to the oven for a further 5-10 minutes until the pizza is crisp and golden brown.

PIZZA TOPPINGS

The quickest and one of the best sauces to use as a base for pizza is passata. This can be bought from most supermarkets in a carton or bottle and is just sieved plum tomatoes. Spread it over the dough, sprinkle with a little good olive oil and season lightly with salt, pepper and some dried oregano or basil before adding your choice of toppings. The quantities given are for each individual pizza.

MARGHERITA
2-3 tablespoons passata, 60g (2 oz) chopped mozzarella cheese, pinch dried oregano, 1 teaspoon olive oil, seasoning.

FLORENTINA
2-3 tablespoons passata, 60g (2 oz) frozen chopped or leaf spinach (thawed), 1 egg, 30g (1 oz) chopped mozzarella cheese, seasoning. Use the spinach to make a border around the pizza, crack the egg into the hollow and sprinkle over the cheese and seasoning.

FUNGHI
2-3 tablespoons passata, pinch dried oregano, 60g (2 oz) sliced mushrooms, 1 chopped garlic clove, 30g (1 oz) chopped mozzarella cheese, 1 teaspoon olive oil, seasoning.

CRESCENT CALAZONE WITH CHEESY POTATOES

EASY!

The Parmesan is rolled into the dough and gives a delicious flavour to the crust. These giant pizza pies will really fill you up, so be prepared to eat well.

Serves 2

500g (1 lb) old potatoes, diced
2 tablespoons milk
125g (4 oz) mature Cheddar, grated
1 small onion, finely chopped
few leaves fresh basil, roughly torn
seasoning
flour for rolling
2 tablespoons freshly grated Parmesan
½ quantity pizza dough (page 23)

1 Cook the potatoes in plenty of boiling salted water for 10-15 minutes until tender. Drain well and mash with the milk until smooth and fluffy. Stir in the cheese, onion, basil and plenty of seasoning.

2 Preheat the oven to 220C,450F, Gas 7. Sprinkle a little flour and the Parmesan onto the work surface. Divide the dough in half and roll out on the work surface into 2 very thin 30 cm (12 inch) rounds. Spoon the cheesy potato onto one side of each of the rounds. Dampen the edges and fold over the dough, pressing with your fingers to seal.

3 Place the calazone on a lightly-oiled baking sheet and bend the 2 corners towards each other to form a crescent shape. Bake for 15-20 minutes until crusty and golden.

VEGETABLE STEW WITH RED WINE AND DUMPLINGS

EASY!

Fortunately vegetable suet is widely available in supermarkets so fluffy dumplings needn't be off the menu.

Serves 2

2 tablespoons olive oil
1 large onion, cut into large pieces
2 garlic cloves, quartered
1 large carrot, thickly sliced
2 parsnips, cut into bite-size pieces
1 leek, thickly sliced
1 tablespoon plain flour
450 ml (¾ pint) vegetable stock
150 ml (¼ pint) red wine
1 tablespoon tomato purée
seasoning
125g (4 oz) button mushrooms

FOR the Dumplings

90g (3 oz) self-raising flour
½ teaspoon salt
30g (1 oz) vegetable suet
1 tablespoon chopped fresh parsley
water to mix

1 Heat the oil in a large saucepan and fry the onion, garlic, carrot, parsnips and leek together for 5 minutes until beginning to turn golden. Sprinkle on the flour and cook for 1 minute.

2 Gradually stir in the stock, wine, tomato purée and seasoning. Bring to the boil, cover and simmer for 10 minutes.

3 Meanwhile, make the dumplings. Sieve the flour and salt into a bowl. Stir in the suet, parsley and 5 tablespoons of water into form a soft dough. Shape into 8 small balls and add to the stew with the mushrooms.

4 Cover and simmer for 20 minutes until the vegetables are tender and the dumplings cooked through. Season to taste and serve immediately.

SANDWICH CALAZONE WITH COURGETTE FILLING

EASY!

This delicious calazone can be cut into squares and eaten cold for a packed lunch. If you want to reheat it, place the squares under a low grill for about 10 minutes until warmed through and crisp.

Serves 2
1 large courgette
1 large onion, finely chopped
2 garlic cloves, finely chopped
2 tablespoons chopped fresh parsley
4 tablespoons olive oil, plus extra for brushing
seasoning
½ quantity pizza dough (page 23)
flour for rolling

1 Preheat the oven to 240C,475F, Gas 9. Quarter the courgettes lengthways then slice very thinly widthways to make little quarter circles. Toss with the onion, garlic, parsley, oil and plenty of seasoning.

2 Divide the dough in half and roll out to make 2 large, thin rectangles about 25cm x 38cm (10 inch x 15 inch). Place one half on a lightly-oiled baking sheet and scatter over the filling, leaving a 1cm (½ inch) border. Dampen the edges and cover with the other rectangle of dough, pressing with your fingers to seal.

3 Brush the top with a little olive oil and bake in the oven for 15-20 minutes until crisp and golden.

MUSHROOM PUFFS

REALLY EASY!

Serve this tasty bread puff with crisp green salad for a simple supper.

Serves 2

2 eggs
7 tablespoons (100 ml) milk
seasoning
2 slices of bread
knob of butter or margarine
1 small onion, finely chopped
1 garlic clove, finely chopped
250g (8 oz) mushrooms, roughly chopped

1 Preheat the oven to 190C, 375F, Gas 5. Beat together the eggs and milk with a little seasoning. Cut the crusts off the bread and tear the bread into small pieces. Add to the eggs and milk and leave to soak for a few minutes.

2 Heat the butter and gently cook the onion and garlic for 5 minutes until softened. Add the mushrooms and cook for a further 2-3 minutes. Season to taste.

3 Add the mushrooms to the bread mixture and stir well together. Transfer to a heatproof dish and cook in the oven for 20-30 minutes until puffed and golden brown.

SPINACH PANCAKES

EASY!

Pancakes are a fantastic base for lots of different meals. This pancake batter has spinach added to it for extra flavour. Try with one of the suggested fillings for a tasty snack or supper dish.

Serves 2
125g (4 oz) plain flour
½ teaspoon salt
1 large egg, beaten
300 ml (½ pint) milk
125g (4 oz) frozen chopped spinach, thawed
vegetable oil for frying

1 Sieve the flour and salt into a large bowl. Make a well in the centre and add the egg and milk. Beat together until smooth. Squeeze the spinach to remove excess water, then stir into the batter.

2 Heat a little oil in a small, shallow, non-stick frying pan. Spoon 2 tablespoons of mixture into the pan and swirl to cover the base. Cook for a few seconds, flip over and cook the second side. Repeat to make 8 pancakes in total.

STUFFING SUGGESTIONS

Try filling the pancakes with one of the suggestions below, roll up, sprinkle over a little grated cheese and heat through under the grill.

Mexican Topping (page 126)

Greek Yogurt with Crispy Onions (page 127)

Feta Cheese with Black Olive Dressing (page 128)

Warm Potato and Mushroom Salad (page 132) with a spoon of hot chilli sauce (page 145)

White Bean Paté (page 142)

Refried Beans (page 153) and sour cream

SPINACH PANCAKES • STUFFING SUGGESTIONS

VEGGIES IN THE HOLE

EASY!

It is important to heat a little oil in the baking dish before you pour in the batter as it creates a seal and prevents sticking.

Serves 2
60g (2 oz) plain flour
seasoning
1 egg, beaten
150 ml (¼ pint) milk
2 tablespoons vegetable oil
1 large onion, sliced
125g (4 oz) baby carrots, scrubbed and trimmed
60g (2oz) frozen peas

1 Preheat the oven to 200C,400F, Gas 6. Sieve the flour into a bowl with a little salt and pepper. Make a well in the centre and pour in the egg and half the milk. Beat to make a stiff batter and gradually work in the remaining milk. Set aside to rest for a few minutes while you fry the vegetables.

2 Heat 1 tablespoon of oil in a large frying pan and cook the onion rings and carrots for 10 minutes until golden. Place remaining tablespoon of oil in a shallow, heatproof dish and place in the oven. When hot remove the dish from the oven and put the carrot and onions into it.

3 Stir the peas into the batter and pour over the vegetables. Bake in the oven for 30 minutes until the batter has risen and is crisp and golden.

WELSH RAREBIT

REALLY EASY!

This method may not be true to the original which is rather time consuming, but it tastes almost as good. Top each slice with a poached egg to make Buck Rarebit.

Serves 1
60g (2 oz) Cheddar, grated
1 teaspoon English mustard
1 tablespoon vegetarian Worcestershire sauce
small knob of butter
2 slices of toast

1 Beat together the cheese, mustard, Worcestershire sauce and butter to make a paste.

2 Spread on the toast and place under the grill for 3 minutes until bubbling and golden.

VEGGIES IN THE HOLE • WELSH RAREBIT

33

FRENCH BREAD CASSEROLE

REALLY EASY!

This is a good way to use up French bread that is a little stale.

Serves 2
3 tablespoons olive oil
1 small onion, finely chopped
1 small aubergine, diced
1 red pepper, diced
1 yellow pepper, diced
400g (14 oz) can plum tomatoes
60g (2 oz) black olives
few leaves fresh basil, roughly torn
seasoning
150g (5 oz) mozzarella, sliced
1 small French stick, thickly sliced

1 Preheat the oven to 220C,425F, Gas 7. Heat 2 tablespoons of the oil in large pan and fry the onion, aubergine and peppers for 5 minutes until golden. Add the tomatoes and juice, olives and basil. Season to taste and simmer, covered, for 15 minutes until the vegetables are tender.

2 Transfer the mixture to an ovenproof dish and scatter over the mozzarella. Carefully arrange the bread slices on top, overlapping them to cover the casserole. Brush or drizzle the remaining oil over the bread and place in the oven for 10-15 minutes until golden brown and crisp.

FATTOUSH

REALLY EASY!

Fattoush is a Lebanese salad that has pieces of crisply toasted pitta bread tossed in just before serving. It make a great lunch in summer.

Serves 2

1 mini cucumber, diced
1 large red pepper, diced
2 firm tomatoes, diced
bunch spring onions, thickly sliced
2 tablespoons chopped fresh parsley
3 pitta breads, toasted until crisp and golden
juice of half a lemon
3 tablespoons olive oil
seasoning

1 Toss together the cucumber, pepper, tomatoes and onions.

2 Break the pittas into bite-size pieces and add to the salad.

3 Whisk together the lemon juice, olive oil and plenty of seasoning. Pour over the salad, toss well together and serve immediately.

MEDITERRANEAN OPEN SANDWICH

REALLY EASY!

All supermarkets and most bakeries now stock ciabatta, the chewy Italian bread made with olive oil. Its firm texture makes it a great base for open sandwiches.

Serves 2

1 loaf of ciabatta bread
60g (2 oz) pitted black olives
1 garlic clove
3 tablespoons olive oil
1 avocado, diced
2 tomatoes, diced
150g (5 oz) mozzarella, diced
6 spring onions, sliced thickly
juice of half a lemon
seasoning

1 Split the loaf in half through the middle. Place the olives and garlic on a board and chop together finely with a heavy knife until blended. Transfer to a small bowl and stir in a tablespoon of the olive oil.

2 Spread the mixture onto the cut surfaces of the bread and place under a hot grill for 3-4 minutes until crisp and golden.

3 Place the avocado, tomatoes, mozzarella, spring onions, remaining olive oil and lemon juice in a bowl. Toss well together and season to taste. Pile on top of the bread and serve immediately.

BEAN AND CHEESE CASSEROLE

EASY!

This bean stew is topped with breadcrumbs and finished in the oven. Try making this dish with any type of beans.

Serves 2

2 tablespoons vegetable oil
1 onion, sliced
2 garlic cloves, chopped
1 celery stick, chopped
400g (14 oz) can mixed beans, drained
200g (7 oz) can chopped tomatoes
½ teaspoon dried mixed herbs
125g (4 oz) cheese, grated
90g (3 oz) fresh breadcrumbs
seasoning

1 Preheat the oven to 190C,375F, Gas 5. Heat one tablespoon of vegetable oil in a large saucepan and gently cook the onion, garlic and celery for 5 minutes until softened. Add the beans, tomatoes, herbs and 150 ml (¼ pint) of water. Season to taste and simmer together for 10 minutes.

2 Transfer half the bean mixture into a casserole dish and place the cheese on top. Spoon over the remaining bean mixture.

3 Sprinkle over the breadcrumbs and bake for 15-20 minutes until golden.

MEDITERRANEAN OPEN SANDWICH • BEAN AND CHEESE CASSEROLE

VEGETABLE SAMOSAS

E·A·S·Y!

These spicy samosas are brilliant for parties.

Makes 8
1 large potato, diced
2 tablespoons vegetable oil
1 small onion, finely chopped
1 hot red chilli, deseeded and finely chopped
1 teaspoon hot curry paste
125g (4 oz) frozen peas, thawed
juice of half a lemon
4 sheets filo pastry

1 Preheat the oven to 220C,425F, Gas 7. Cook the potato in boiling, salted water for 10-12 minutes until just tender. Drain well.

2 Heat the oil in a large frying pan and cook the onion, chilli and curry paste for 2-3 minutes. Add the potatoes and peas and cook for a further 2-3 minutes, mashing down lightly with a fork. Remove from the heat. Stir in the lemon juice.

3 Work with 1 sheet of pastry at a time, keeping the rest covered with a damp cloth. Cut each sheet in half lengthwise to give 2 long strips. Put a spoon of the mixture in one corner of each strip.

4 Fold pastry and filling over at right angles to make a triangle and continue folding in this way along the strip of pastry to form a neat triangular parcel. Repeat with remaining mixture.

5 Place on a baking sheet and brush with a little extra oil. Bake in the oven for 10-15 minutes until crisp and golden. Eat hot or cold.

SESAME NAAN WITH CORIANDER

E A S Y !

Impress your friends with your own, home-made bumper naan breads.

Serves 2

250g (8 oz) self raising flour
3 tablespoons live natural yogurt
1 teaspoon easy-blend dried yeast
½-1 teaspoon finely chopped fresh coriander
1 teaspoon salt
1-2 tablespoons sesame seeds
small knob of butter

1 Mix the flour, yeast, coriander and salt together in a large bowl and make a well in the centre. Spoon in the yogurt and gradually add about 6 tablespoons of warm water, bringing the mixture together to form a very soft, slightly sticky dough. Knead lightly for 1 minute then cover with a tea-towel and leave in a warm place for about an hour.

2 Preheat the grill to high. Divide the dough into 2 equal pieces and roll out on a lightly floured surface into two large rectangles, each as big as your grill pan. Press sesame seeds into both sides of each Naan. Roll lightly with a rolling pin to press well in. Place under the grill for about 1 minute on the first side and 30 seconds on the other, until puffed and lightly browned. When the naans are ready, and still hot, spread them with a little butter.

FRYING PAN PIZZA

REALLY EASY!

If you fancy a pizza just for yourself, but don't have the time or energy for making up some bread dough, this delicious frying-pan pizza is quick, simple and just as tasty.

Serves 1
125g (4 oz) self-raising flour
pinch salt
water to mix
2 tablespoons olive oil

1 Place the flour and salt in a bowl. Make a well in centre and add 3 tablespoons of water and 1 table-spoon of olive oil. Mix together to make a firm dough.

2 Shape the mixture into a ball and then flatten or roll out to fit a small frying pan. Heat the remaining oil in the pan and fry the pizza base for about 5 minutes until golden brown.

3 Flip over and cook the other side for 5 minutes, slide onto a plate and serve with a topping of your choice, eg. a fried egg and halved tomato. Alternatively, cover the uncooked top with a cheesy mixture (see below) and place under a hot grill for 5 minutes until bubbling and golden. Eat immediately.

35

CHEESY TOPPINGS

- Cream cheese and chopped fresh herbs

- Sliced Cheddar and tomatoes

- 2 tablespoons passata sprinkled with grated Cheddar

- Grated cheese mixed with butter and mustard

- Mushrooms fried in butter and garlic sprinkled with grated cheese

- Mozzarella and slivers of sundried tomato

- Small can of baked beans topped with grated Cheddar

CREAMY VEGETABLE TURNOVERS

EASY!

You can make these pasties with any vegetables, why not try making a cauliflower cheese version.

Makes 4

1 large carrot, diced
60g (2 oz) frozen peas
125g (4 oz) small broccoli florets
knob of butter
1 tablespoon plain flour
300 ml (½ pint) milk, plus extra for brushing
1 tablespoon chopped fresh parsley
seasoning
250g (8 oz) ready-made puff pastry, thawed if frozen

1 Preheat the oven to 220C, 425F, Gas 7. Place the carrots, peas and broccoli in a metal sieve and sit over a pan of boiling water. Cover with a lid or foil and steam gently for 5 minutes until tender but still crisp.

2 Meanwhile, melt the butter in a small pan. Stir in the flour and cook for 1 minute. Gradually beat in the milk to make a smooth sauce. Bring to the boil and simmer for 2 minutes until thickened. Stir the vegetables, parsley and seasoning into the sauce. Allow to cool.

3 Roll the pastry into 15cm (6 inch) squares and spoon in the vegetable mixture. Dampen the edges and fold over the pastry to form triangles, pressing down the edges to seal.

4 Transfer to a baking sheet and brush with a little milk Place in the oven for 15-20 minutes until puffed and golden brown. Serve with salad or vegetables.

FETA AND TOMATO PASTIES

EASY!

Why not make double the recipe – these little pasties are good for a packed lunch.

Serves 2

250g (8 oz) ready made puff pastry, thawed if frozen
180g (6 oz) Feta cheese, crumbled
1 large tomato, skinned, seeded and chopped
1 tablespoon chopped fresh parsley or chives
1 egg
2 tablespoons milk
seasoning

1 Preheat the oven to 220C,425F, Gas 7. Roll the pastry out into a large rectangle, measuring 30cm x 15cm (12 inch x 6 inch). Cut in half to give two 15cm (6 inch) squares.

2 Sprinkle the cheese on one half of each square and season well. Top with the chopped tomato and herbs. Beat together the egg and milk and brush a little around the edges. Fold over to make a triangle and press down well along the edges to seal.

3 Transfer to a baking sheet and brush all over with the egg. Place in the oven for 15-20 minutes until puffed and golden. Serve with salad or vegetables.

BAKED BEAN AND CHEESE FLAN

REALLY EASY!

This dish takes only minutes to prepare but is filling and tasty. Serve with a big helping of mashed potato.

Serves 2

400g (14 oz) can baked beans
20 cm (8 inch) shortcrust pastry case
150 ml (¼ pint) milk
1 egg
seasoning
60g (2 oz) Cheddar, grated

1 Preheat the oven to 190C, 375F, Gas 5. Tip the can of beans into the pastry case.

2 Beat together the milk, egg and a little seasoning. Pour over the beans. Sprinkle the cheese on top and bake in the oven for 25-35 minutes, until set.

EGGY BREAD SANDWICH

REALLY EASY!

Use any filling you like for this sandwich but cheese works particularly well. The secret of eggy bread is to leave the bread soaking in the egg for as long as you can; 20 minutes is ideal. If you have any egg mixture left over, pour it on top of the bread as it is cooking in the pan.

Serves 1

60g (2 oz) grated cheese
1 tablespoon mayonnaise
1 spring onion, finely chopped (optional)
2 slices of white bread
1 egg
2 tablespoons milk
seasoning
vegetable oil for frying

1 Mix together the cheese, mayonnaise and onion and spread thickly on a slice of the bread. Top with the other slice to make a sandwich.

2 Beat the egg, milk and a little seasoning together in a shallow dish and lay in the sandwich. Press down with a spatula so the bread absorbs the liquid.

3 Heat a little oil a frying pan and cook the bread for 3-4 minutes on each side until puffed and golden brown. Drain on kitchen paper and eat straightaway.

BAKED BEAN AND CHEESE FLAN • EGGY BREAD SANDWICH

CHEESY CRUST CASSEROLE

EASY!

Aubergine, courgette and pepper with tomatoes, topped with a delicious cheesy crust. The pastry top is very easy to make and if you don't have a rolling pin, try using a clean jar or bottle or pat out with your hands.

Serves 2

2 tablespoons olive oil
1 onion, roughly chopped
2 garlic cloves, finely chopped
1 small courgette, thickly sliced
1 small aubergine, cubed
1 yellow pepper, diced
400g (14 oz) can chopped tomatoes and their juice
1 teaspoon dried thyme
seasoning

For The Cheese Crust

90g (3 oz) self-raising flour
½ teaspoon salt
30g (1 oz) vegetable suet
60g (2 oz) Cheddar, finely grated
water to mix

1 Preheat the oven to 200C,400F, Gas 6. Heat the oil in a large frying pan and stir-fry the onion, garlic, courgette, aubergine and pepper for about 8 minutes until softened and beginning to brown. Add the tomatoes and thyme and season to taste. Simmer gently for 10 minutes.

2 Meanwhile place the ingredients for the crust into a large bowl. Add 5 tablespoons of cold water and bring to together to form a soft dough. Roll out on a lightly floured surface until large enough to cover your casserole dish.

3 Transfer the tomato mixture to a small casserole dish and lay the dough on top. Press the dough around the edges with your thumbs. Bake for 25 minutes until puffed and golden brown.

TOMATO TART

EASY!

**It is very important that the mozzarella is well
drained or the water will soak through the tart
and make the pastry soggy.**

Serves 2

*250g (8 oz) ready-made puff pastry, thawed if frozen
2 tablespoons ready-made pesto sauce
2 large tomatoes, thinly sliced
salt and freshly ground black pepper
handful of basil leaves
150g (5 oz) mozzarella cheese*

1 Preheat the oven to 220C,425F, Gas 7. Roll the pastry out into a large rectangle, about 5 mm (¼ inch) thick. Using a small sharp knife, cut a border about 1 cm (½ inch) wide inside the rectangle – cut deep into the pastry, but not right through.

2 Spread the pesto sauce within the border and arrange the tomatoes on top. Season generously and scatter with the basil leaves. Drain the mozzarella well on kitchen paper and slice as thinly as possible.

3 Arrange the mozzarella slices on top of the tart and carefully transfer to a baking sheet. Place in the oven for 15-20 minutes until the border has risen up to provide a puffy golden rim to the tart. Serve hot with a crisp green salad.

HERBY SAUSAGES

REALLY EASY!

**These veggie sausages keep well in the fridge;
simply cover and chill for a day or two
before cooking.**

Serves 2
90g (3 oz) fresh white breadcrumbs
60g (2 oz) Cheddar, grated
1 tablespoon freshly grated Parmesan
4 tablespoons chopped fresh chives
1 teaspoon English mustard
1 teaspoon dried sage
1 egg
seasoning
2 tablespoons plain flour
vegetable oil for frying

1 Mix together the breadcrumbs, cheeses, chives, mustard, sage, egg and plenty of seasoning.

2 With floured hands, shape the mixture into 4 sausages.

3 Heat a little oil in a small frying pan and cook for 5-8 minutes until golden brown.

TOMATO TART • HERBY SAUSAGES

PASTA

Pasta is simply flour blended into a firm dough with water and eggs. It is fairly easy to make fresh pasta yourself but it is relatively time-consuming and when there are so many varieties of pasta you can buy cheaply and cook in a few minutes, you can be forgiven for opting for dried or ready-made fresh pasta.

DRIED OR FRESH?

There are some people who claim that fresh pasta is superior to the dried. I don't agree, they are both equally good depending upon the sort of dish you want to create. Dried pasta is very cheap, can be stored easily for a long time and is firm with a good bite. If, however, you fancy a filled pasta such as ravioli or tortellini, there are some very exciting fresh types around such as tomato ravioli filled with salmon and dill, that are well worth splashing out a little extra on for a special occasion. They usually cook in less than 5 minutes and just need tossing with a little warm cream for a super quick, but sophisticated supper.

COOKING

Pasta should be cooked in as a large a pan as possible so that it can move around freely and cook evenly. Bring a large pan of salted water to a rolling boil and toss in the pasta, stir once and cook rapidly until tender with a firm bite. If you're cooking filled pasta shapes, the water should simmer quite gently so that the parcels do not burst open.

PASTA OMELETTE

REALLY EASY!

This is a great way of using left over pasta – even pasta that has been coated in a tomato or cheese sauce works well in an omelette. Serve with salad or baked beans for a complete meal.

Serves 1
1 tablespoon olive oil
1 garlic clove, sliced
60g (2 oz) cooked pasta shapes
2 eggs
2 tablespoons milk
1 tablespoon chopped fresh parsley or 1 teaspoon dried seasoning
30g (1 oz) Cheddar, grated

1 Heat the oil in a small frying pan and stir fry the garlic and pasta for 3-4 minutes until heated through.

2 Beat together the eggs, milk, parsley and a little seasoning. Pour over the pasta and cook gently for 3-4 minutes until the egg is almost set on top and golden brown underneath.

3 Sprinkle over the cheese and place under a hot grill for 2-3 minutes until golden and bubbling. Slide onto a plate and serve immediately.

CREAMY MUSHROOM PASTA

REALLY EASY!

Always use double cream for this recipe as you can boil it without fear of it curdling.

Serves 2
250g (8 oz) pasta shapes
small knob of butter or margarine
1 large garlic clove, finely chopped
180g (6 oz) large flat mushrooms, sliced
150 ml (¼ pint) double cream
1 tablespoon chopped fresh parsley
seasoning
1 tablespoon freshly grated Parmesan

1 Cook the pasta in plenty of boiling water for 10-12 minutes or until tender.

2 Meanwhile, heat the butter in a small saucepan and gently cook the garlic and mushrooms for 5 minutes. Add the cream, parsley and season to taste. Bring to the boil and simmer gently for 3 minutes.

3 Drain the pasta well and toss together with the sauce. Divide into serving bowls and sprinkle over the Parmesan. Serve immediately.

PASTA OMELETTE • CREAMY MUSHROOM PASTA

ROSY SPIRALS

REALLY EASY!

You will find cartons of creamed or sieved tomatoes in any supermarket, usually positioned near the tomato purée. Or if you have a 400g (14 oz) can of chopped tomatoes handy, pass through a sieve and use instead.

Serves 2

250g (8 oz) pasta spirals
500g (1lb) carton creamed tomatoes
90g (3 oz) pack garlic and herb flavoured soft cheese,
e.g. Boursin
½ teaspoon sugar
salt and freshly ground black pepper
1 tablespoon chopped fresh parsley

1 Cook the pasta in plenty of boiling water for 10-12 minutes or until tender.

2 Meanwhile, place the creamed tomatoes and soft cheese in a small saucepan. Heat together gently for 5-6 minutes, stirring until the cheese has melted and the sauce has warmed through. Season to taste and stir in the parsley.

3 Drain the pasta well and toss together with the sauce. Divide into bowls and serve with a sprinkling of freshly ground black pepper.

TAGLIATELLE WITH PARSLEY PESTO

REALLY EASY!

This is a cheaper, but just as tasty a version of the classic basil and pine nut pesto. Why not have go at trying this dish with different combinations of herbs and nuts.

Serves 2
2 handfuls of fresh parsley (flat leaf if possible)
2 tablespoons shelled pistachios or walnuts
2 garlic cloves
2 tablespoons olive oil
60g (2 oz) butter, softened
60g (2 oz) freshly grated Parmesan
250g (8 oz) pasta ribbons
seasoning

1 Place a big pan of salted water on to boil. Use a heavy knife to finely chop together the parsley, nuts and garlic cloves, until well blended. Place the mixture in a small bowl and stir in the oil, butter and Parmesan.

2 When the water is boiling, toss in the pasta and cook until tender. Scoop out 2 tablespoons of hot water from the pasta pan and add to the pesto mixture. Drain the pasta and return to the pan.

3 Add the pesto and toss well together until thoroughly mixed. Season to taste and serve immediately with a little extra Parmesan scattered on top.

ROSY SPIRALS • TAGLIATELLE WITH PARSLEY PESTO

PASTA NAPOLITANA

E A S Y !

This is a classic tomato sauce. It tastes really good simply tossed with spaghetti and served with a sprinkling of Parmesan.

Serves 2

Napolitana Sauce
2 tablespoons olive oil
1 onion, finely chopped
2 garlic cloves, finely chopped
400g (14 oz) can chopped tomatoes, and their juice
1 tablespoon tomato purée
1 teaspoon dried oregano
pinch of sugar
seasoning

250g (8 oz) pasta
1 tablespoon freshly grated Parmesan, to serve

1 To make the sauce, heat the oil in a saucepan and gently cook the onion and garlic for 5 minutes until softened. Add the tomatoes, purée, oregano, sugar and seasoning. Bring to the boil and simmer very gently, uncovered for about 30 minutes until thick and pulpy.

2 Meanwhile cook the pasta in plenty of boiling, salted water for 10-12 minutes or until tender. Drain and return to the pan. Add about half of the sauce to the pasta and toss well together to mix.

3 Divide into 2 serving bowls and spoon the remaining sauce over the pasta. Sprinkle with Parmesan and serve immediately.

MINESTRONE SOUP

REALLY EASY!

Don't feel tied to this recipe. Chop and change the vegetables as you wish. The word 'minestrone' simply means big soup, but it almost always has pasta in it. Use pastina, tiny pasta shapes specially made for soups, or break strands of spaghetti into very short lengths.

Serves 2-3
1 tablespoon olive oil
60g (2 oz) mushrooms, chopped
1 small onion, chopped
1 garlic clove, chopped
1 carrot, diced
1 courgette, diced
1 small potato, diced
1 celery stick, diced
2 tomatoes, diced
900 ml (1½ pints) vegetable stock
60g (2 oz) pastina
1 tablespoon chopped fresh parsley
1 tablespoon freshly grated Parmesan
seasoning

1 Heat the olive oil in a large saucepan. Fry together the mushrooms, onion, garlic, carrot, courgette, potato and celery for 5 minutes. Add the tomatoes and stock, cover and simmer for 1 hour.

2 Stir in the pastina and parsley and cook for 10 minutes until pastina is tender. Check seasoning, ladle into bowls, sprinkle with Parmesan and serve.

SPAGHETTI WITH VODKA AND CHILLI

REALLY EASY!

This is a very trendy dish but it really does taste delicious – use extra oil if you don't have any butter but I wouldn't recommend substituting the vodka with any other spirit.

Serves 2

250g (8 oz) spaghetti
1 tablespoon of olive oil
small knob of butter
2 small chillies, deseeded and finely chopped
2 tomatoes, skinned, deseeded and finely chopped
4 tablespoons vodka
4 tablespoons double cream
salt and freshly ground black pepper
freshly grated Parmesan, to serve

1 Cook the pasta in plenty of boiling water for 10-12 minutes or until tender.

2 Meanwhile, heat the oil and butter in a small frying pan, add the chillies and tomatoes and cook for 4 minutes. Add the vodka and simmer rapidly for about 3 minutes. Stir in the cream, bring to the boil and remove from the heat. Season to taste.

3 Drain the pasta well and toss with sauce. Divide into bowls and serve sprinkled with Parmesan and freshly ground black pepper.

PASTA FAGOLI

REALLY EASY!

**This is a traditional Southern Italian dish –
'fagoli' meaning beans.**

Serves 2
2 tablespoons olive oil
1 onion, roughly chopped
2 garlic cloves, finely chopped
600 ml (1 pint) vegetable stock
400g (14 oz) can cannellini beans, drained
200g (7 oz) can chopped tomatoes, drained
125g (4 oz) small pasta shapes
4 tablespoons chopped fresh parsley
seasoning

1 Heat the oil in a large saucepan and cook the onion and garlic for 5 minutes until softened.

2 Add the stock, beans and tomatoes and simmer together for 10 minutes. Add the pasta and cook for a further 10-15 minutes until tender.

3 Stir in the parsley and season to taste. Serve immediately.

SPAGHETTI WITH VODKA AND CHILLI • PASTA FAGOLI

RIGATONI WITH AUBERGINES

REALLY EASY!

A pasta sauce made with vegetable chunks is best paired with large pasta shapes such as rigatoni (tubes), shells or quills rather than ribbons.

Serves 2

250g (8 oz) pasta tubes
1 large aubergine weighing around 350g (12 oz)
5 tablespoons olive oil
2 garlic cloves, sliced
big handful fresh basil or parsley, roughly chopped
3 tablespoons freshly grated Parmesan, plus extra to serve
salt and freshly ground black pepper

1 Cook the pasta in plenty of boiling water for 10-12 minutes or until tender.

2 Meanwhile, cut the aubergine into sticks about 2.5 cm (1 inch) long and 5 mm (¼ inch) thick. Heat the oil in a large frying pan and stir fry the aubergine and garlic for 7 minutes until softened and golden.

3 Drain the pasta well and add to the frying pan. Stir in the herbs, Parmesan and plenty of seasoning. Divide into bowls and serve immediately with a little extra Parmesan sprinkled over.

PASTA ALFREDO

REALLY EASY!

**One of the fastest pasta dishes you can make –
great when you're really hungry.**

Serves 2
250g (8 oz) tagliatelle
4 tablespoons double cream
1 egg
*2 tablespoons freshly grated Parmesan, plus extra to
serve*
salt and freshly ground pepper
60g (2 oz) butter, cut into small pieces

1 Cook the pasta in plenty of salted boiling water for
10-12 minutes or until tender.

2 Beat together the cream, egg, Parmesan and plenty
of seasoning. Drain the pasta well and return to the
pan. Add the cream mixture and butter and toss well
together. Divide into bowls and serve immediately with
a little extra Parmesan sprinkled over.

RIGATONI WITH AUBERGINES • PASTA ALFREDO

CHEESY PASTA PUFF

EASY!

This cheese soufflé is another great way of using up leftover pasta.

Serves 2-3

180g (6 oz) macaroni, or other small pasta shapes
60g (2 oz) butter or margarine
60g (2 oz) plain flour
300 ml (½ pint) milk
1 teaspoon English mustard
125g (4 oz) Cheddar, grated
seasoning
3 eggs, separated
1 tablespoon freshly grated Parmesan

1 Cook the pasta in plenty of boiling water for 10-12 minutes or until tender. Drain well and set aside to cool. Preheat the oven to 180C,350F, Gas 4.

2 Melt the butter in a saucepan, add the flour and cook, stirring, for 1 minute. Gradually beat in the milk to make a smooth sauce. Stir in the mustard, Cheddar and plenty of seasoning. Bring to the boil, stirring until the cheese melts. Set aside for 5 minutes to cool.

3 Stir the pasta and egg yolks into the sauce. In a separate bowl, whisk the egg whites until stiff and carefully fold into the pasta mixture.

4 Spoon into a greased heatproof dish and sprinkle over the Parmesan. Bake in the oven for 40-45 minutes until puffed and golden brown. If the topping browns too quickly, cover with foil. Serve immediately with crisp green salad.

MACARONI WITH BROCCOLI, LEMON AND BLUE CHEESE

REALLY EASY!

Pre-packed broccoli in supermarkets can often be quite expensive, so if you are near any market stalls, always check out the price – you'll find it is often cheaper and you can buy the exact amount you want.

Serves 2
180g (6 oz) macaroni
250g (8 oz) broccoli florets
knob of butter or margarine
1 tablespoon flour
200 ml (7 fl oz) vegetable stock
seasoning
grated rind and juice of half a lemon
60g (2 oz) blue cheese, crumbled

1 Cook the pasta in plenty of lightly salted boiling water for 7 minutes. Add the broccoli to the pan and cook together for a further 5 minutes until both pasta and broccoli are tender.

2 Meanwhile, heat the butter in a small pan, add the flour and beat together with a wooden spoon until smooth. Gradually stir in the stock, bring to the boil and season to taste. Add the lemon juice and rind and simmer gently for 1 minute.

3 Drain the pasta and broccoli. Put in a dish and pour over the sauce. Sprinkle over the blue cheese and toss well together and serve.

CHEESY PASTA PUFF • MACARONI WITH BROCCOLI, LEMON AND BLUE CHEESE

SPAGHETTI MARINARA

REALLY EASY!

Buy capers pickled in a vinegar from most supermarkets. They will keep in the fridge for a quite a while and are great for topping pizzas.

Serves 2

2 tablespoons olive oil, plus extra to serve
1 onion, finely chopped
2 garlic cloves, thinly sliced
2 tablespoons roughly torn basil
400g (14 oz) can chopped tomatoes and their juice
125g (4 oz) pitted black olives, halved
1 tablespoon capers
salt and freshly ground black pepper
250g (8 oz) spaghetti

1 Heat the oil in a saucepan and gently cook the onion, garlic and basil for 5 minutes until softened. Add the tomatoes, cover and simmer for 15 minutes.

2 Meanwhile cook the pasta in plenty of boiling, salted water for 10-12 minutes or until tender.

3 Add the olives and capers to the tomatoes and season to taste. Drain the pasta and return to the pan. Add about half of the sauce to the pasta and toss well together to mix.

4 Divide into 2 serving bowls and spoon the remaining sauce over the pasta. Drizzle with a little extra olive oil and sprinkle with some freshly ground black pepper. Eat immediately.

GARLIC OIL SPAGHETTI

REALLY EASY!

This is strictly for true garlic fans. If you wish, add a sliced fresh or small dry chilli with the garlic.

Serves 2
250g (8 oz) spaghetti
4 tablespoons olive oil
6 garlic cloves, thickly sliced
salt and freshly ground black pepper

1 Cook the pasta in plenty of boiling water for 10-12 minutes or until tender.

2 Meanwhile heat the oil in a small saucepan. Add the garlic and fry gently for 3-4 minutes, until golden, taking care not to burn the garlic. Remove the garlic.

3 Drain the pasta and return to the pan. Add the flavoured oil and toss well together. Season generously adding a little hot water or more oil if the pasta seems dry. Serve immediately.

SPAGHETTI MARINARA • GARLIC OIL SPAGHETTI

PASTA PRIMAVERA

E A S Y !

Primavera means spring and this dish is traditionally made with spring vegetables such as asparagus, courgettes and fresh peas.

Serves 2
2 tomatoes, quartered
3 tablespoons olive oil
1 onion, sliced
1 garlic clove, finely chopped
125g (4 oz) frozen peas
1 courgette, sliced
2 tablespoons chopped fresh parsley
180g (6 oz) pasta shapes

1 Place a big pan of salted water onto boil. Arrange the tomatoes skin side up on a baking sheet and brush with a little of the olive oil. Cook for about 8 minutes under a preheated grill, turning once, until golden brown and a little charred.

2 While the tomatoes are grilling, heat the remaining oil in a saucepan and gently cook the onion and garlic for 10 minutes until softened and lightly golden.

3 Cook the pasta for 10-12 minutes or until tender. Meanwhile, add the grilled tomatoes, peas and courgettes to the pan of onions. Season well, cover and cook gently for 5-10 minutes, until the pasta is cooked.

4 Drain the pasta well and toss with the vegetables and parsley. Serve immediately.

THREE-CHEESE SAUCE WITH PISTACHIOS

REALLY EASY!

This is a sauce recipe to serve over any pasta of your choice. To save buying large pieces of cheese, look out for individual packs in the 'Pick and Mix' sections of some supermarkets.

Serves 2

125 ml (4 fl oz) single cream
45g (1½ oz) Gorgonzola, crumbled
45g (1½ oz) grated fresh Parmesan
30g (1 oz) grated Gruyère cheese
30g (1 oz) shelled pistachio nuts, chopped
1 teaspoon finely chopped basil
ground white pepper
180g (6 oz) pasta, cooked

1 Put cream into a saucepan and bring slowly to the boil. Reduce heat, add Gorgonzola cheese and stir until melted and smooth. Stir in Parmesan and Gruyère cheeses. Cook over a low heat, stirring constantly, until sauce is thick and smooth.

2 Add the pistachio nuts and basil. Season to taste with pepper. To serve, pour over hot cooked pasta of your choice.

BAKED PEPPER PASTA

REALLY EASY!

Grilled peppers tossed with pasta, tomatoes, herbs and mozzarella.

Serves 2

250g (8 oz) pasta shapes
1 large red pepper, deseeded and quartered
1 large orange pepper, deseeded and quartered
1 tablespoon olive oil
2 garlic cloves finely chopped
2 tablespoon roughly chopped fresh basil or 1 teaspoon dried
400g (14 oz) can chopped tomatoes, drained
150g (5 oz) mozzarella, diced
seasoning
2 tablespoons freshly grated Parmesan

1 Preheat the oven to 200C,400F, Gas 6. Cook the pasta in plenty of boiling salted water for 10-12 minutes or until tender. Drain.

2 Meanwhile, brush the peppers with oil and place under a preheated grill for 8 minutes, turning once, until tender. Cut into bite-size pieces.

3 Toss together the pasta, peppers, garlic, basil, tomatoes and mozzarella. Season to taste and spoon into a greased ovenproof dish. Sprinkle with the Parmesan and bake in the oven for 15-20 minutes until heated through and golden brown on top.

BROCCOLI PASTA

REALLY EASY!

All parts of broccoli are edible – peel the juicy stalk with a potato peeler or sharp knife and slice into thin rounds.

Serves 2

180g (6 oz) pasta shapes eg bows, shells
180g (6 oz) broccoli, cut into small florets
4 tablespoons olive oil
2 garlic cloves, thinly sliced
1 red onion, finely chopped
1 small red chilli, deseeded and finely chopped
seasoning
2 tablespoons freshly grated Parmesan

1 Cook the pasta in plenty of salted boiling water for 8 minutes. Add the broccoli to the pan and cook for a further 4 minutes until the pasta and vegetables are tender.

2 Meanwhile, heat the oil in a small frying pan and gently cook the garlic, onion, chilli and seasoning for 5 minutes until softened.

3 Drain the pasta well and toss with onion mixture. Divide into serving bowls and sprinkle with Parmesan. Serve immediately.

BAKED PEPPER PASTA • BROCCOLI PASTA

PASTA AND LENTIL SOUP

EASY!

**There's nothing quite as comforting as soup
and this one is very tasty and filling on
a cold winter's night.**

Serves 2-3

*1 tablespoon olive oil, plus extra to serve
2 celery sticks, finely chopped
1 small onion, finely chopped
1 garlic clove, finely chopped
2 tablespoons chopped fresh parsley
1.15 litres (2 pints) vegetable stock
1 tablespoon tomato purée
1 small potato, peeled and diced
2 tomatoes, diced
60g (2 oz) brown or green lentils
60g (2 oz) small pasta shapes
salt and freshly ground black pepper.*

1 Heat the oil in a large saucepan and cook the celery, onion, garlic and parsley for 5 minutes until softened.

2 Add the stock, tomato purée, diced potato and tomatoes and the lentils. Bring to the boil and simmer gently for 30 minutes. Add the pasta and cook for a further 10-15 minutes until the lentils and pasta are tender.

3 Season to taste and divide into bowls. Serve with a swirl of olive oil and a good sprinkling of freshly ground black pepper.

HAZELNUT PASTA

REALLY EASY!

A lovely pasta dish flavoured with garlic, Parmesan and hazelnuts.

Serves 2

250g (8 oz) pasta shapes
4 tablespoons olive oil
2 garlic cloves, roughly chopped
125g (4 oz) hazelnuts, roughly chopped
3 tablespoons freshly grated Parmesan
seasoning

1 Cook the pasta in plenty of boiling water for 10-12 minutes or until tender.

2 Meanwhile, heat the oil in small frying pan and gently cook the garlic and hazelnuts for about 5 minutes until lightly golden.

3 Drain the pasta well and toss with the hazelnut mixture, Parmesan and plenty of seasoning. Serve immediately.

RICE AND GRAINS

Cheap, nutritious and very easy to cook, rice is
the staple diet in many countries. It thrives on
waterlogged, marshy soil where other cereals,
such as wheat will not grow.

INTRODUCTION

Although there are literally hundreds of different rices, there are only 2 basic grains, long and round. Round rice is stirred during cooking to release the starch and produce a creamy, slightly sticky rice which is perfect for things like milk puddings, risottos or sushi. Long grain rices stay separate and should be washed well before cooking and not stirred whilst being cooked.

COOKING RICE

There are two very good methods of boiling long grain rice. I normally go for the straight forward Open Pan method but the Absorption technique is just as successful.

Open Pan Method

Bring a large pan of salted boiling water to the boil. Tip in the rice, stir once and simmer fairly rapidly, uncovered, until the rice is tender. Drain in a sieve and turn out onto a large plate for 2 minutes to allow the grains to dry and separate.

Absorption Method

After weighing the rice it tip into a measuring jug or a mug and take note of the volume before transferring to a saucepan. Now measure twice that volume in cold water and add to the pan with a teaspoon of salt. Bring to the boil, lower the heat to a slow simmer, cover tightly and cook for 15-20 minutes for long grain rice, 10 minutes for basmati and 35-45 minutes for brown.

RICE TYPES
Risotto rice
Risotto rice is a plump, longish, round grain that absorbs lots of liquid and cooks easily without becoming mushy. If stirred frequently during cooking, it gives a very creamy texture. The best risotto rice is Arborio. It is a bit expensive and in my experience all the risotto rices are good.

Long grain white rice
This is a polished rice that, like most other white rices including risotto and basmati, has had its husk and bran removed. It can be boiled using either of the two methods above or used for biryani or other oven baked savoury rices where separate grains are preferred.

Basmati rice
This is a very delicate, long, slim, fragrant grain that is used extensively in Indian cookery. It is relatively expensive and can be replaced by the usual long grain rice if preferred. It should be washed very well several times and soaked in warm water for 20 minutes before cooking. After soaking it must be handled carefully as the grains are fragile and can easily break. Cook by either of the methods described for just 10 minutes or use for aromatic pilau or spiced rice dishes.

Brown rice

Brown rice is a long grain rice which has only had the very tough husk removed, and the bran left intact. It has a nutty flavour and quite chewy texture. Because of the tough layer it takes about 45 minutes to cook and absorbs a lot more water than white. It is however, not only one of the most flavoursome rices but also the most nutritious.

There are lots of other grains and cereals that are used for cooking worldwide. Experiment with different grains, both whole and milled see Chick-pea and Tomato Couscous (page 76) and Bulgar Wheat Salad with Soft Cheese Dressing (page 80) for more ideas.

CHICK-PEA AND TOMATO COUSCOUS

EASY!

If you're feeling flush, add the cashew nuts to this dish, if not, use peanuts or leave them out altogether.

Serves 2

180g (6 oz) couscous
2 tablespoons vegetable oil
1 onion, roughly chopped
1 garlic clove, finely chopped
1 cm (½ inch) piece fresh root ginger, peeled and finely chopped
½ teaspoon ground cumin
4 tomatoes, skinned and roughly chopped
150 ml (¼ pint) vegetable stock
400g (14 oz) can chick-peas, drained
4 tablespoons Greek yogurt
1 tablespoon chopped fresh coriander
60g (2 oz) cashew nuts (optional)
seasoning

1 Put the couscous in a bowl and cover with boiling water for 10 minutes until it has swollen.

2 Meanwhile, heat the oil in a saucepan and cook the onion, garlic, ginger and cumin for 5 minutes until softened. Stir in the tomatoes, vegetable stock and chick-peas and bring to the boil.

3 Line a metal sieve with a new J cloth or a very clean tea towel and place over the pan. Tip in the couscous. Cover the pan with foil, to enclose the steam and simmer very gently for 15 minutes until the stew is thickened and the couscous is piping hot.

4 Fluff up the couscous with a fork and divide onto plates. Stir the yogurt, chopped coriander and nuts if using, into the stew and season to taste. Spoon onto the bed of couscous and serve.

CHICK-PEA AND TOMATO COUSCOUS

JANE'S
PEANUT NOODLES

REALLY EASY!

Vegetarian student Jane who is my flatmate, manages to include peanut butter in just about every dish she cooks. In this recipe it tastes delicious.

Serves 2

125g (4 oz) Chinese egg noodles
1 tablespoon vegetable oil
1 onion, roughly chopped
1 garlic clove, thinly sliced
1 hot red chilli, deseeded and finely chopped
1 carrot, sliced
125g (4 oz) button mushrooms, halved
3 tablespoons crunchy peanut butter
60g (2 oz) creamed coconut
1 tablespoon soy sauce
2 tablespoons water
125g (4 oz) frozen leaf spinach, thawed
seasoning

1 Cook the noodles according to packet instructions, drain and set aside.

2 Meanwhile, heat the oil in a wok or large frying pan and stir-fry the onion, garlic, chilli, carrot and mushrooms for 5 minutes until beginning to brown.

3 Add the peanut butter, creamed coconut, soy sauce and water, and cook for a further 2-3 minutes until the vegetables are tender.

4 Stir in the spinach and noodles and season to taste. Heat through for 1-2 minutes until piping hot and serve immediately.

HOT TOMATO RISOTTO

REALLY EASY!

A creamy risotto with tomatoes, garlic and chillies.

Serves 2

1 tablespoon olive oil
small onion, finely chopped
1 garlic clove, crushed
2 hot red chillies, deseeded and finely chopped
250g (8 oz) risotto rice
400g (14 oz) can of chopped tomatoes and their juice
900 ml (1½ pints) vegetable stock
4 tomatoes, skinned and roughly chopped
30g (1 oz) butter
2 tablespoons freshly grated Parmesan
2 tablespoons chopped, fresh parsley

1 Heat the oil in a large pan and gently fry the onion, garlic and chillies for 5 minutes until softened. Stir in the rice and cook together for a further 1 minute.

2 Tip in the can of tomatoes and stir until the juices are absorbed by the rice. Gradually add the stock a little at a time, waiting for the liquid to be absorbed before adding any more, until the rice is cooked. Cook the rice over a fairly high heat stirring frequently. It should take around 20 minutes to absorb the liquid.

3 When the rice is cooked, stir in the fresh chopped tomatoes, butter, Parmesan and parsley and season to taste. Serve immediately.

BULGAR WHEAT SALAD WITH SOFT CHEESE DRESSING

REALLY EASY!

Eat this crunchy salad with pitta bread for a light lunch or supper or if you're really hungry, serve as an accompaniment to Seedy Bean Burgers (page 109) or Stuffed Mushrooms (page 112).

Serves 2
125g (4 oz) bulgar wheat
1 green pepper, deseeded and cut into small dice
1 large carrot, cut into small dice
1 garlic clove, finely chopped
1 onion, finely chopped
125g (4 oz) packet of peanuts and raisins
60g (2 oz) soft cheese
juice of a lemon
3 tablespoons olive oil
seasoning

1 Put the bulgar wheat in a large bowl and fill with boiling water. Set aside for 20 minutes until the grains have swollen and absorbed most of the water. Drain well and return to the bowl.

2 Stir in the pepper, carrot, garlic, onion, peanuts and raisins, mixing well together. Spoon onto serving plates.

3 Whisk together the soft cheese, lemon juice, olive oil and seasoning and drizzle over the salad.

EGG AND LEMON SOUP

EASY!

This is a classic Greek rice soup. Unlike the Chinese-style egg soups, the idea is not to have strands of egg, but to cook them gently so they thicken the soup without scrambling.

Serves 2
600 ml (1 pint) vegetable stock
60g (2 oz) long grain rice
2 eggs
juice of a lemon
seasoning
1 tablespoon chopped fresh parsley

1 Place the stock in a large saucepan and bring to the boil. Add the rice, cover and cook for 15-20 minutes until the rice is tender.

2 Whisk the eggs until frothy, then mix in the lemon juice and a ladle of the hot stock.

3 Turn the heat down low, and slowly pour in the egg mixture, stirring constantly until slightly thickened. Take care not to boil the soup or the eggs will curdle.

4 Season to taste and stir in the parsley. Serve immediately.

ORANGE RICE

REALLY EASY!

For extra flavour, toast the peanuts for a few minutes under a hot grill, stirring occasionally until golden.

Serves 2
2 tablespoons vegetable oil
1 small onion, finely chopped
1 carrot, cut into small dice
250g (8 oz) long grain rice
juice and finely grated rind of 2 large oranges
450 ml (¾ pint) vegetable stock
60g (2 oz) frozen peas
60g (2 oz) frozen sweetcorn
60g (2 oz) salted peanuts
1 tablespoon chopped fresh parsley
seasoning

1 Heat the oil in a large saucepan and cook the onion and carrot for 5 minutes until beginning to turn golden brown. Add the rice and cook for a further 1 minute.

2 Add the orange juice and vegetable stock. Cover and simmer for 10 minutes.

3 Stir in the peas and sweetcorn and continue to cook for a further 5 minutes until the rice and vegetables are tender.

4 Add the peanuts, parsley and orange rind. Check the seasoning and serve.

CARROT AND COURGETTE RICE PATTIES

EASY!

This a great way to use up leftover rice. The patties are quite crumbly when being shaped but once in the pan, they cook beautifully with a crunchy coating and soft, melting inside.

Serves 2
180g (6 oz) cooked long grain rice
1 courgette, finely grated
1 carrot, finely grated
60g (2 oz) finely grated Gruyère or Cheddar
1 garlic clove, crushed
1 tablespoon chopped fresh parsley
3 tablespoons plain flour
2 eggs
seasoning
6 tablespoons fresh breadcrumbs
vegetable oil for frying

1 Stir together the rice, courgette, carrot, cheese, garlic, parsley, 1 tablespoon of flour, 1 beaten egg and plenty of seasoning.

2 Shape into 6 round, flat patties. Coat in flour, then in egg and finally breadcrumbs.

3 Heat 2.5 cm (1 inch) of oil in a small deep frying pan and cook the patties for 3-4 minutes on each side, until golden brown. Drain on kitchen paper and serve with tomato ketchup or Hot Chilli Sauce (page 145) and salad.

ORANGE RICE • CARROT AND COURGETTE RICE PATTIES

MUSHROOM AND EGG PILAU

EASY!

Rice with onion and mushrooms, flavoured with curry and mango chutney with sliced omelette stirred in at the end.

Serves 2

2 tablespoons vegetable oil
1 small onion, chopped
1 teaspoon hot curry paste
250g (8 oz) mushrooms, thickly sliced
250g (8 oz) long grain rice
450 ml (¾ pint) vegetable stock
1 tablespoon mango chutney
2 eggs, beaten
1 garlic clove, finely chopped
1 tablespoon finely chopped coriander
seasoning

1 Heat a tablespoon of the oil in a large saucepan with a close-fitting lid. Cook the onion and curry paste for 5 minutes until softened. Add the mushrooms and rice and cook for a further 1 minute.

2 Pour in the stock and chutney and bring to the boil. Stir once, then cover and simmer very gently for 20 minutes.

3 Meanwhile, beat together the eggs, garlic, coriander and a little seasoning. Heat a little of the remaining oil in a small frying pan and pour in the eggs. Cook gently until golden brown underneath and almost set. Flip over and cook the second side.

4 Cut the thick omelette into bite-size pieces and when the rice is tender, fork into the pilau. Season to taste and serve.

VEGETARIAN JAMBALAYA

REALLY EASY!

**Jambalaya has no rules, try adding different
vegetables for an equally tasy result.**

Serves 2
1 tablespoon vegetable oil
1 garlic clove
1 onion, chopped
1 small hot chilli, chopped
1 red pepper, diced
2 sticks celery, thickly sliced
60g (2 oz) tiny button mushrooms
150g (5 oz) long grain white rice
2 large tomatoes, diced
300 ml (½ pint) vegetable stock
2 tablespoons chopped fresh parsley
seasoning

1 Heat the oil in a large pan and gently cook the garlic, onion, chilli, pepper and celery for 5 minutes, until softened.

2 Add the mushrooms, rice, tomatoes and stock, bring to the boil, cover and simmer for 15-20 minutes until the rice is tender and the liquid has been absorbed.

3 Stir in the parsley and season to taste. Serve immediately.

MUSHROOM AND EGG PILAU • VEGETARIAN JAMBALAYA

CHINESE EGG-FRIED RICE

REALLY EASY!

The secret of egg-fried rice is to cook the egg separately. If you add raw egg to the hot rice whilst in the pan, it will absorb the egg and become sticky.

Serves 2
2 tablespoons vegetable oil
2 eggs, beaten
1 garlic clove, finely chopped
2.5 cm (1 inch) piece fresh root ginger, finely chopped
1 red pepper, deseeded and diced
1 carrot, cut into matchsticks
60g (2 oz) frozen peas
6 spring onions, thickly sliced
250g (8 oz) cooked long grain rice
1 tablespoon soy sauce

1 Heat a little oil in a wok or large frying pan. Tip in the beaten eggs and stir with a chopstick until set. Remove from the wok and set aside.

2 Heat the remaining oil in the pan and stir-fry the garlic, ginger, pepper and carrot over a high heat for 5 minutes.

3 Stir in the peas, spring onions, rice and egg and continue to cook, stirring for a further 3-5 minutes, until piping hot. Season with the soy sauce and serve.

RICE AND LENTILS

REALLY EASY!

**This is a brilliant emergency dish that you can
make almost entirely with store cupboard
ingredients. If you're really broke, you can
make it with just onions, rice and lentils.**

Serves 2
*2 tablespoons vegetable oil
1 large onion, chopped
2 garlic cloves, finely chopped
2 sticks celery, chopped
1 small red chilli, deseeded and finely chopped
250g (8 oz) long grain rice
180g (6 oz) red lentils
2 tomatoes, skinned and chopped
900 ml (1½ pints) vegetable stock
seasoning*

1 Heat the oil in a large pan and cook the onion, garlic, celery and chilli for 5 minutes until softened. Add the rice and cook for a further 1 minute.

2 Stir in the lentils, tomatoes and stock. Bring to the boil, cover and simmer for 15-20 minutes until the rice and lentils are tender. Do not stir the rice but check it to make sure it hasn't boiled dry, adding more stock or water if necessary.

3 Season to taste, spoon onto plates and serve.

TABBOULEH

R E A L L Y   E A S Y !

**This classic Lebanese salad is based on
bulgar wheat, also labelled as cracked wheat.
When you buy it in the shops, it has already
been cooked and then dried so it just needs
rehydrating with a little boiling water. Keep it
cool and dry in your cupboard and it will last
for months.The addition of Greek feta cheese
makes tabbouleh taste even better. Eat with
warm pitta bread or use it to stuff hollowed-
out beef tomatoes.**

Serves 2

125g (4 oz) bulgar wheat
2 tomatoes, chopped
4 spring onions, sliced
125g (4 oz) feta cheese, crumbled or diced
2-3 tablespoons finely chopped parsley
juice of a lemon
3 tablespoons olive oil
seasoning

1 Put the bulgar wheat in a large bowl and fill with
boiling water. Set aside for 20 minutes until the grains
have swollen and absorbed most of the water. Drain
very well and return to the bowl.

2 Stir in the tomatoes, onions, feta, parsley, lemon
juice and olive oil. Mix well together, season to taste
and serve.

PESTO AUBERGINES WITH BULGAR WHEAT

REALLY EASY!

Serve the aubergines on your choice of cooked grain – couscous also works very well.

Serves 2
125g (4 oz) bulgar wheat
1 large aubergine
1 tablespoon olive oil
2 tomatoes, skinned and finely diced
1 tablespoon freshly grated Parmesan

For the Dressing
2 tablespoons purchased pesto sauce
2 tablespoons olive oil
juice of a half a lemon
salt and freshly ground black pepper

1 Put the bulgar wheat in a large bowl and fill with boiling water. Set aside for 20 minutes until the grains have swollen and absorbed most of the water. Drain.

2 Slice the aubergines lengthwise into 1 cm (½ inch) thick slices. Brush with oil and place under a preheated grill for 6-10 minutes until golden and tender.

3 Spoon the warm bulgar wheat onto plates and arrange the aubergine slices on top. Sprinkle over the tomatoes and scatter with the Parmesan.

4 Whisk together the pesto, olive oil, lemon juice, a little salt and plenty of black pepper. Drizzle the dressing over the aubergines and serve while still warm.

SOUPY VEGETABLE RICE

R E A L L Y   E A S Y !

**If you want to keep half of this economical dish
in the fridge to eat the following day, you may
need to add a little extra stock as the rice
will absorb a lot of the liquid when it's
left to stand.**

Serves 2

1 tablespoon olive oil
1 onion, finely chopped
2 garlic cloves, finely chopped
1 carrot, finely diced
1 potato, finely diced
60g (2 oz) long grain rice
600 ml (1 pint) vegetable stock
2 tomatoes, skinned and finely chopped
60g (2 oz) frozen peas
1 tablespoon tomato ketchup
2 tablespoons chopped fresh parsley
seasoning

1 Heat the oil in a large pan and cook the onion, garlic, carrot and potato for 5 minutes until beginning to turn golden brown. Stir in the rice and cook for 1 minute.

2 Add the stock, bring to the boil and simmer for 10 minutes. Add the tomatoes and peas and simmer for a further 5-10 minutes until the rice and vegetables are tender.

3 Stir in the ketchup and parsley and season to taste. Divide into bowls and serve.

(35)

CARIBBEAN RICE

REALLY EASY!

An exotic flavoured rice dish with ginger, chilli, pineapple, coconut and almonds.

Serves 2

1 tablespoon vegetable oil
1 large onion, sliced
1 teaspoon finely grated root ginger
1 small red chilli, deseeded and finely chopped
250g (8 oz) long grain rice
200g (7 oz) can pineapple chunks in natural juice
450 ml (¾ pint) vegetable stock
1 tablespoon dessicated coconut (optional)
seasoning
1 tablespoon chopped fresh parsley
1 tablespoon toasted flaked almonds

1 Heat the oil in a large saucepan and cook the onion, ginger and chilli for 10 minutes until softened and golden brown. Add the rice and cook for 1 minute.

2 Stir in the pineapple chunks with the juice, the vegetable stock, coconut, if using and seasoning. Bring to the boil, stir once, cover and simmer gently for 20 minutes until the grains are tender.

3 Gently stir in the parsley and almonds and serve immediately.

VEGETABLE PAELLA

R E A L L Y   E A S Y !

Paella always contains saffron, which is incredibly expensive. This vegetarian version uses turmeric which adds a wonderful colour and its own flavour to the dish. Of course it is not same as using the real thing but it's a very good substitute.

Serves 2
2 tablespoons olive oil
1 small onion, chopped
1 garlic clove, finely chopped
1 large carrot, diced
1 red pepper, deseeded and diced
1 small aubergine, diced
1 teaspoon turmeric
250g (8 oz) long grain rice
600 ml (1 pint) vegetable stock
½ teaspoon dried thyme
seasoning
2 tomatoes, skinned and roughly chopped
60g (2 oz) frozen peas

1 Heat the oil in a large pan and fry the onion and garlic for 5 minutes until softened. Add the carrot, pepper, aubergine and turmeric and cook gently for a further 5 minutes.

2 Add the rice and cook for 1 minute. Stir in the stock, thyme and seasoning and bring to the boil. Cover and simmer gently, without stirring, for 10 minutes.

3 Gently stir in the tomatoes and peas and cook for a further 10 minutes until the rice and vegetables are tender. Spoon onto plates and serve.

VEGETABLES

AND BEANS

This food group is so immense with shapes, colours, sizes and flavours stretching across the whole spectrum. You are sure to see different odd-looking vegetables each time you venture out to the shops as the range of imported goods becomes wider and more varied each day. Once you've mastered home-grown produce you might like to start experimenting with dishes that involve something more exotic, but for the moment stick to what you know.

INTRODUCTION

EAT SEASONALLY

It makes sense to base your meals around what's in season. Fresh fruit and vegetables in the peak of their season have far more flavour than those imported from hotter climates or grown in greenhouses to meet out of season demand. Not only do seasonal vegetables taste better, they're also a lot cheaper. Here's a quick guide to when fruits and vegetables are at their seasonal best, and cheapest to buy.

January – avocados, sweet potatoes

February – lemons, limes, pink grapefruit, marrows

March – broccoli, white cabbage, spring greens

April – cauliflower, cucumber, radishes, mushrooms

May – new potatoes, asparagus, spring greens, spinach, rhubarb

June – courgettes, peas, mangetout, salad lettuces, broad beans, strawberries, watercress

July – peppers, runner beans, globe artichokes, currants, peaches, nectarines

August – corn on the cob, celery, pak choi, aubergines, blackberries, apricots

September – marrows and squashes, plums

October – red cabbage, parsnips, swedes, potatoes, turnips, pumpkins, apples, pears

November – leeks, shallots, Brussels' sprouts, oranges

December – beetroot, cabbages (red and white) Jerusalem artichokes, nuts, figs

SHOPPING
Buy fresh fruit and vegetables from your local market, if you can, because the prices will be substantially lower than in the supermarket or corner shop, and if you shop on the way home from college, you're sure to pick up some end-of-day bargains. As mentioned in the Eating Well chapter, it is best not to store fresh vegetables for too long so don't buy in bulk. If you only need two carrots, don't feel you have to buy a whole pound.

BEANS
It is very cheap and easy to buy dried beans and soak and cook them yourself, but it means you have to plan your meal at least a day in advance. There is such a

fantastic range of inexpensive canned beans to be found on the shelves of supermarkets, that I'm not sure how many people actually take the time to cook dried beans. But for those of you who do want to, it is very important that you follow this guide carefully as certain beans, particularly kidney beans, contain toxins that can make you quite ill if they are not destroyed by cooking:

1 Place the beans in a sieve or colander and rinse well, remove any pieces of grit. Tip into a large bowl, fill with cold water and leave for 8 hours, or overnight to soak. Don't soak for over 24 hours or the beans will start to ferment.

2 Rinse well and place in a large saucepan. Cover with cold water, bring to the boil and boil rapidly for 15 minutes.

3 Drain and rinse well. Place in a saucepan and cover with clean cold water, bring to the boil and simmer, uncovered, for 1-1½ hours until tender. Don't add salt as it can toughen the beans.

PEPPERONATA

REALLY EASY!

Serve this with crusty bread to mop up the juices or try tossing with freshly cooked pasta or using to top a baked potato.

Serves 1
4 tablespoons of olive oil
1 red pepper, deseeded and sliced
1 yellow pepper, deseeded and sliced
1 large onion, sliced
2 garlic cloves, sliced
2 tomatoes, skinned and quartered
1 tablespoon chopped fresh basil or parsley
salt and freshly ground black pepper

1 Heat the oil in a saucepan and add the peppers, onion and garlic. Cover and simmer very gently, stirring occasionally, for 25 minutes until the vegetables are softened.

2 Add the tomatoes and cook for a further 15 minutes until tender. Stir in the parsley and season to taste. Serve hot or at room temperature.

CAULIFLOWER TORTILLA

REALLY EASY!

Spanish tortillas always contain potatoes, so although this does not technically qualify, it's every bit as tasty.

Serves 2
250g (8 oz) cauliflower florets
2 tablespoons olive oil
125g (4 oz) frozen peas
1 small red chilli, deseeded and finely chopped
1 garlic clove, finely chopped
4 eggs, beaten
2 tablespoons milk
1 tablespoon chopped fresh parsley or 1 teaspoon dried seasoning

1 Plunge the cauliflower florets into boiling salted water for 3-4 minutes until just tender but still crisp. Drain.

2 Heat the oil in a small deep frying pan and cook the peas, chilli and garlic together for 5 minutes until soft. Add the cauliflower and stir-fry for 2-3 minutes.

3 Beat together the eggs, milk, parsley and seasoning. Pour over the vegetables, turn down the heat to the lowest setting and cook gently for about 8 minutes until the mixture is almost completely set – keep checking the underside to make sure it doesn't burn.

4 Use a fish slice to carefully turn the tortilla over, or if it's a little tricky, place a plate over the pan, invert the tortilla onto the plate and then slide it back into the pan. Cook for a further 2 or 3 minutes until the underside is golden brown. Cut into wedges and serve.

SPICY BEAN BURGERS

EASY!

Burgers made with butterbeans and spinach and flavoured with garlic, cumin, and tahini.

Serves 2
1 tablespoon vegetable oil
1 small onion, finely chopped
2 garlic cloves, finely chopped
400g (14 oz) can butterbeans
125g (4 oz) frozen chopped spinach, thawed
60g (2 oz) fresh breadcrumbs
1 teaspoon ground cumin
1 tablespoon tahini
seasoning

1 Heat the oil in a small saucepan and fry the onion and garlic for 5 minutes until softened.

2 Mash the beans well and place in a bowl with the spinach, breadcrumbs, cumin and tahini. Add the fried onion mixture and stir well together.

3 Season to taste and shape into four round burgers. Grill or shallow fry for a few minutes on each side until crisp and golden. Serve in burger buns with relish and salad.

SPINACH AND CHICK-PEA SOUP

REALLY EASY!

Serves this hearty soup with thick slices of buttered toast for a filling meal.

Serves 2

2 tablespoons olive oil
1 large onion, sliced
1 small red chilli, deseeded and diced
600 ml (1 pint) vegetable stock
250g (8 oz) frozen leaf spinach
2 tomatoes, skinned and diced
400g (14 oz) can chick-peas, drained
salt and freshly ground black pepper

1 Heat the oil in a large saucepan, add the onion and chilli and cook for 5 minutes until softened. Add the stock, spinach, tomatoes and chick-peas and bring to the boil. Cover and simmer for 15 minutes.

2 Season to taste and ladle into bowls. Serve with a swirl of olive oil and a good sprinkling of freshly ground black pepper.

BAKED BEAN AND LEEK HASH

REALLY EASY!

Baked beans are a stand-by in almost everyone's cupboard and they make a great addition to this hash.

Serves 2

2 tablespoons vegetable oil
500g (1 lb) potatoes, diced
1 large leek, finely chopped
400g (14 oz) can baked beans
60g (2 oz) Cheddar, grated
seasoning

1 Heat the oil in a large heavy-based frying pan. Add the potatoes, and cook, stirring, for 10 minutes, until semi-cooked.

2 Add the leeks, and continue to cook for 5 minutes, stirring, until the leeks have softened.

3 Stir in the beans, grated cheese and seasoning and cook the hash over a medium heat, until a crust forms on the bottom. Stir the hash to let the mixture brown throughout.

4 Turn the hash over, and pat down to form a cake. Cook until a crust forms on the bottom. Turn onto plates and serve.

CHINESE-STYLE MIXED MUSHROOMS

REALLY EASY!

A wonderfully quick and very tasty stir-fry of mushrooms. Serve with Chinese Egg-Fried Rice (page 86).

Serves 2

1 tablespoon vegetable oil
1 hot red chilli, thinly sliced
2 garlic cloves, thinly sliced
1 bunch spring onions, thickly sliced on the diagonal
250g (8 oz) mixed mushrooms (shitake, oyster, chanterelles etc.)
2 tablespoons soy sauce
4 tablespoons dry cider
150 ml (¼ pint) hot vegetable stock
1 teaspoon sesame oil
1 teaspoon cornflour
½ teaspoon five spice powder

1 Heat the vegetable oil in a wok or large frying pan. Add the chilli, garlic, spring onions and mushrooms and stir-fry over a high heat for 3 minutes.

2 Blend together the soy sauce, cider, stock, sesame oil, cornflour and five spice powder and pour over the mushrooms. Bring to the boil and simmer for 3 minutes until the mushrooms are just tender and the sauce has thickened. Serve immediately on a bed of egg-fried rice.

CHEESE AND ONION SOUP

REALLY EASY!

A creamy rich soup made with onions, cheese and mustard.

Serves 2

small knob of butter
1 large onion, chopped
1 tablespoon plain flour
600 ml (1 pint) milk
125g (4 oz) mature Cheddar, grated
1 tablespoon wholegrain mustard
seasoning

1 Melt the butter in a large pan and cook the onion for 10 minutes until softened and golden. Stir in the flour and cook for 1 minute.

2 Gradually beat in the milk and bring to the boil. Stir in the cheese and mustard and simmer gently for 2-3 minutes until the cheese has melted. Season to taste and serve with hot buttered toast or warm crusty bread.

CHINESE-STYLE MIXED MUSHROOMS • CHEESE AND ONION SOUP

PAN FRIED COURGETTES WITH EGGS AND PARMESAN

EASY!

When poaching eggs, the vinegar is added to the water to help prevent the white spreading out too much. If you prefer you can top this dish with soft-boiled eggs in place of the poached.

Serves 1

2 tablespoons olive oil
1 courgette, cut into sticks about 7.5 x 1 cm (3 x ½ inch)
1 large field or open cup mushroom, sliced
seasoning
1 tablespoon vinegar
2 eggs
1 tablespoon mayonnaise
30g (1 oz) Parmesan, sliced thinly with a vegetable peeler

1 Heat the oil in a large frying pan and when sizzling add the vegetables. Stir-fry over a high heat for 3-4 minutes until golden. Season well and transfer to a warm plate.

2 Half fill a small frying pan with water, add the vinegar and bring to the boil. Crack an egg into a cup and carefully slide it into the pan, repeat with the other egg. Poach for 3-4 minutes until the whites have set. Scoop out with a slotted spoon and drain on kitchen paper.

3 Spoon the mayonnaise onto the vegetables and top with the poached eggs. Scatter over the Parmesan and serve immediately.

VEGETABLE SATAY

REALLY EASY!

Satay sauce usually contains coconut and can be quite complicated to make. This is an easy short-cut version which tastes great on almost any grilled vegetable.

Serves 2
1 courgette, thickly sliced
2 tomatoes, quartered
1 red pepper, deseeded and cut into 2.5 cm (1 inch) pieces
1 yellow pepper, deseeded and cut into 2.5 cm (1 inch) pieces
125g (4 oz) small broccoli florets
1 tablespoon vegetable oil
seasoning

For the Satay Sauce
4 tablespoons smooth peanut butter
1 tablespoon vegetarian Worcestershire sauce
3 tablespoons boiling water.

1 Thread the vegetables onto skewers and brush lightly with oil. Season and place under a preheated grill for about 10 minutes, turning occasionally, until tender.

2 Mix together the peanut butter and Worcestershire sauce and stir in the boiling water. Drizzle over the vegetable kebabs and serve on a bed of rice or with pitta bread and salad.

MULLIGATAWNY

REALLY EASY!

This spicy curry soup is sure to brighten up a rainy day.

Serves 2

2 tablespoons vegetable oil
1 garlic clove, finely chopped
1 onion, finely chopped
1 potato, cut into small dice
1 large carrot, cut into small dice
1 tablespoon curry paste
60g (2 oz) red lentils
600 ml (1 pint) vegetable stock
60g (2 oz) ground almonds
seasoning

1 Heat the oil in a large saucepan. Add the garlic, onion, potato and carrot and cook for 5 minutes until beginning to turn golden brown.

2 Stir in the curry paste, lentils and stock. Bring to the boil, cover and simmer for 20 minutes, stirring occasionally, until the vegetables and lentils are tender.

3 Mix the almonds with little water to form a paste and add to the soup. Season to taste and serve immediately.

VEGETABLE KORMA

REALLY EASY!

**This is great way of making use of leftover
cooked vegetables – simply reduce the cooking
time at step 2 to 5 minutes.**

Serves 2

1 tablespoon vegetable oil
1 onion, finely chopped
1 tablespoon curry paste
500g (1 lb) mixed vegetables cut into bite-size chunks
e.g. carrot, potato, broccoli, cauliflower. peas
400 ml (14 fl oz) can coconut milk
60g (2 oz) flaked almonds
seasoning

1 Heat the oil in a large saucepan and cook the onion over a fairly high heat for 5 minutes until golden brown. Stir in the curry paste and cook for 1 minute.

2 Add the vegetables and coconut milk, cover and simmer for 15 minutes until the vegetables are tender. Meanwhile, place the almonds in a non-stick frying pan and dry-fry for 2-3 minutes, tossing the almonds until golden brown.

3 Season the curry to taste and sprinkle over the toasted almonds. Serve immediately with rice or naan bread.

MULLIGATAWNY • VEGETABLE KORMA

CREAMY RED PEPPER SOUP

REALLY EASY!

This sweet, rich soup is so simple to make but tastes very sophisticated. Why not serve it to friends or for a special occasion. Try it with orange or yellow peppers for a change.

Serves 2

2 red peppers, quartered and deseeded
2 tomatoes, halved
750 ml (1¼ pints) vegetable stock
150g (5 oz) carton Greek yogurt
1 tablespoon chopped fresh coriander or parsley
seasoning

1 Arrange the peppers and tomatoes on a baking sheet and place under a preheated grill for 8 minutes, turning once, until softened. Carefully peel the skins from the peppers and tomatoes and discard.

2 Roughly chop the grilled vegetables and place in a saucepan with the stock. Cover and simmer for 20 minutes then push through a metal sieve.

3 Return to the pan and add the yogurt and coriander. Heat through without boiling, season to taste and serve with warm crusty bread.

SEEDY BEAN BURGERS

REALLY EASY!

Fried pumpkin seeds have a delicious smoky flavour. For a tasty snack, dry-fry a handful in a non-stick pan for 2-3 minutes until golden and season with salt. Do watch out as they have a tendency to fly out of the pan as they get hot!

Serves 2
1 tablespoon vegetable oil
3 tablespoons pumpkin seeds
1 onion, finely chopped
1 small red chilli, deseeded and finely chopped
400g (14 oz) can cannellini beans, drained and mashed
60g (2 oz) fresh breadcrumbs
1 egg, beaten
1 tablespoon lemon juice
2 tablespoons chopped fresh parsley
seasoning
vegetable oil for frying

1 Heat the oil in a large frying pan and gently cook the pumpkin seeds, onion and chilli for 5 minutes. Remove from the heat. Stir in the beans, breadcrumbs, egg, lemon juice, parsley and seasoning.

2 Using floured hands, shape into 4 flat patties and shallow fry for 3-4 minutes on each side until crisp and golden brown. Remove with a slotted spoon and drain on kitchen paper. Serve in a bun with salad and mayonnaise or eat with ketchup and chips.

CREAMY RED PEPPER SOUP • SEEDY BEAN BURGERS

MEXICAN CHILLI

REALLY EASY!

Red kidney beans with onion, tomatoes, chilli and oregano – best served with rice.

Serves 2
1 tablespoon vegetable oil
1 onion, finely chopped
1-2 red chillies, deseeded and finely chopped
1 garlic clove, finely chopped
1 tablespoon paprika
1 teaspoon chilli powder
1 tablespoon tomato purée
400g (14 oz) can red kidney beans, drained
200g (7 oz) can chopped tomatoes and their juice
1 teaspoon dried oregano
seasoning

1 Heat the oil in large pan and cook the onion, chillies and garlic for 5 minutes until softened and lightly golden. Add the paprika and chilli powder and cook for 1 minute.

2 Stir in the tomato purée, beans, chopped tomatoes and oregano. Cover and simmer gently for 10 minutes. Season to taste and serve with rice.

EGGS FLORENTINE

EASY!

Eggs baked in the oven on a bed of creamy spinach.

Serves 1
knob of butter
1 small onion, finely chopped
1 tablespoon plain flour
300 ml (½ pint) milk
125g (4 oz) frozen chopped spinach, thawed
1 tomato, skinned and roughly chopped
2 eggs
seasoning

1 Preheat the oven to 200C,400F, Gas 6. Heat the butter in a pan and gently cook the onion for 5 minutes until softened. Stir in the flour and cook for 1 minute.

2 Gradually beat in the milk to make a smooth sauce. Bring to the boil and simmer for 2-3 minutes until thickened. Stir in the spinach and tomato and season to taste.

3 Pour the mixture into a small heatproof dish and make 2 hollows. Crack an egg into each hollow and sprinkle over some freshly ground black pepper. Bake in the oven for 10-15 minutes until the eggs have set. Serve immediately with crusty bread.

MEXICAN CHILLI • EGGS FLORENTINE

STUFFED MUSHROOMS

REALLY EASY!

Large flat mushrooms baked in the oven with a topping of creamy garlic cheese, walnuts, parsley and breadcrumbs.

Serves 1

125g (4 oz) soft cheese with garlic and herbs, e.g. Boursin
2 tablespoons chopped fresh parsley
1 tablespoon chopped walnuts
2 tablespoons fresh breadcrumbs
seasoning
2 large field mushrooms

1 Preheat the oven to 200C, 400F, Gas 6. Stir together the soft cheese, parsley, walnuts and breadcrumbs and season to taste.

2 Place the mushrooms on a baking sheet and pile the cheese mixture on top. Cook in the oven for 20 minutes until tender and golden. Serve immediately with a crisp salad.

TOFU STIR-FRY

EASY!

If the tofu is too wet it will crumble into the stir-fry rather than keep its shape, so it must be drained well. If you have a little more time, try deep frying the cubes of tofu before adding to the stir-fry, for a crispy, chewy texture.

Serves 2

300g (10 oz) packet firm tofu
1-2 tablespoons vegetable oil
1 garlic clove, finely chopped
1 cm (½ inch) piece fresh root ginger, peeled and finely chopped
250g (8 oz) broccoli, cut into small florets
1 red pepper, deseeded and cut into 2.5 cm (1 inch) pieces
1 tablespoon soy sauce

1 Remove the tofu from the packet and place on 2 layers of kitchen paper. Put 2 more sheets on top and weigh down for 5 minutes with a saucepan or heavy chopping board. Cut into about twelve 2.5 cm (1 inch) cubes.

2 Heat the oil in a wok or large frying pan, add the garlic, ginger, broccoli and red pepper and stir-fry over a high heat for 4 minutes.

3 Add the tofu and cook for a further 3-4 minutes until the vegetables are tender but still crisp. Season with the soy sauce and serve immediately with noodles or rice.

BAKED AUBERGINES

EASY!

**If you don't have time to make the tomato
sauce yourself, use one of the many
commercial brands available.**

Serves 2
1 tablespoon vegetable oil
seasoning
2 eggs, beaten
1 large aubergine, sliced into 1 cm (½ inch) rounds
1 quantity of Napolitana sauce (page 56)
150g (5 oz) mozzarella cheese, sliced
1 tablespoon freshly grated Parmesan

1 Preheat the oven to 180C,350F, Gas 4. Heat the oil in a large frying pan. Season the eggs. Dip the aubergine slices in the beaten egg. Fry for 2-3 minutes on each side until golden brown. Remove with a slotted spoon and drain on kitchen paper.

2 Pour half the tomato sauce into a deep ovenproof dish and arrange a layer of aubergines on top. Scatter over the mozzarella and top with the remaining aubergine rounds. Pour over the rest of the tomato sauce and sprinkle with Parmesan. Bake in the oven for 30 minutes until golden and bubbling.

CAULIFLOWER CHEESE

REALLY EASY!

The secret of a good cauliflower cheese is to make sure that the cauliflower is not overcooked – it should be firm and even slightly crunchy rather than soft.

Serves 2
1 cauliflower, cut into florets
30g (1 oz) butter or margarine
30g (1 oz) plain flour
300 ml (½ pint) milk
180g (6 oz) mature Cheddar, grated
1 teaspoon English mustard
seasoning

1 Place the florets in a colander and sit over a pan of boiling water. Cover with a lid or foil and steam for 5-7 minutes, until tender, but not mushy.

2 Meanwhile, melt the butter in a pan, stir in the flour and cook for 1 minute. Gradually beat in the milk to make a smooth sauce. If it does become lumpy, whisk it vigorously.

3 Bring the sauce gently to the boil and add about ¾ of the cheese and the mustard. Simmer for 1-2 minutes, until the cheese has melted and season to taste.

4 Transfer the cauliflower to a heatproof dish and pour over the cheese sauce. Scatter over the remaining cheese and place under a hot grill for 5 minutes until golden and bubbling.

BAKED AUBERGINES • CAULIFLOWER CHEESE

115

BAKED COURGETTES

EASY!

Halved courgettes filled with onion, chilli, sweetcorn, cream and Parmesan and baked in the oven.

Serves 2

4 courgettes
1 tablespoon vegetable oil
1 small onion, finely chopped
1 small chilli, deseeded and finely chopped
180g (6 oz) sweetcorn
1 egg, beaten
1 tablespoon chopped fresh parsley
4 tablespoons double cream
2 tablespoons freshly grated Parmesan
salt and freshly ground black pepper

1 Preheat the oven to 180C, 350F, Gas 4. Halve the courgettes, scoop out the seeds with a teaspoon and discard. Arrange the courgettes side by side in a small ovenproof dish, cut side up.

2 Heat the oil in small pan and very gently cook the onion and chilli for about 5 minutes, until softened. Stir in the sweetcorn, egg, parsley, cream, Parmesan, and a little salt and plenty of black pepper.

3 Spoon the mixture over the courgettes and bake in the oven for 30 minutes until golden brown. Serve with salad and crusty bread.

CRISPY PARSNIP CAKES

REALLY EASY!

Although the idea of boiled parsnips isn't everyone's cup of tea, these crispy patties really do taste brilliant.

Serves 2

4 large parsnips, peeled and cubed
knob of butter
1 teaspoon mild curry paste
seasoning
2 tablespoons plain flour
1 egg, beaten
60g (2 oz) fresh breadcrumbs
vegetable oil for frying

1 Boil the parsnips in lightly salted boiling water for 10-15 minutes until tender. Drain well and mash with the butter, curry paste and seasoning. Leave to cool.

2 Shape into 4 round patties. Season the flour lightly and use to coat the patties. Dip them in the egg and then coat with the breadcrumbs.

3 Fry in hot oil for 3-4 minutes on each side until crisp and golden brown. Drain on kitchen paper and serve immediately with baked beans or crisp green salad.

BAKED COURGETTES • CRISPY PARSNIP CAKES

POTATOES

There are basically two types of potato, new and old. Although new potatoes are available all year, they are at their best in the spring. Small, waxy and firm they are thin skinned and should be eaten soon after buying. They taste delicious steamed, boiled or stir-fried in olive oil. Old potatoes are thicker skinned and are from the second harvest of the year. They are hardy enough to stand longer lengths of storage and are great for roasting, baking, mashing and making chips.

INTRODUCTION

Don't buy or eat potatoes that have turned green. Cut out any eyes, and sprouting, blackened or bruised areas from the potatoes before you cook them. Store them in a brown paper bag in your food cupboard or some other cool, dark, dry place.

Boiling

If using old potatoes, peel or scrub them well, cutting out all blemishes. Cut into quarters and place in a large saucepan. Cover with cold salted water and bring to the boil. Simmer for about 20 minutes or so until tender. If you are boiling potatoes for mash, use old ones and cut them into small pieces to speed up the cooking time. If you're boiling new potatoes, scrub them well, but don't peel. Plunge them into salted boiling water and cook for 10-20 minutes, depending upon their size, until tender.

Baking

See Classic Baked Potato on page 123.

Roasting

Preheat the oven to 190C,375F, Gas 5. Place 3-4 tablespoons of vegetable oil in a roasting tin and put in the oven to heat. Peel the potatoes and cut into quarters, put into the tin with a sprinkle of salt and toss well with the hot oil. Roast for about 1-1½ hours, turning occasionally, until crisp on the outside and soft and fluffy on the inside. If you want to speed up the cooking time, boil the potatoes for about 8 minutes before roasting. Add flavour to roast potatoes by cooking them with a couple of whole garlic cloves and a sprig of fresh herbs such as rosemary or sage.

Making Chips

The best way to cook chips is to fry them twice. If you're going to make your own chips, it's well worth the trouble of doing it properly, as it is the only way to get good crisp chips that are also soft and fluffy inside. Scrub the potatoes in clean cold water and cut into fingers as thick or thin as you like. Wash well, rinsing off excess starch to stop them sticking together, and dry thoroughly with kitchen paper. Heat a couple of inches of vegetable oil in a small deep frying pan until a cube of bread turns brown in about a minute. Cook the chips for 5 minutes or until pale golden. Remove with a slotted spoon and drain on kitchen paper. Raise the heat slightly and when the oil is hot enough to brown a cube of bread in 30 seconds, return the chips to the pan for 1-2 minutes, until crisp. Drain on kitchen paper and sprinkle with salt.

CREAMY POTATO GRATIN

REALLY EASY!

Although this gratin takes a long time to cook in the oven, the actual preparation of the dish won't take more than 15 minutes. Serve with a juicy tomato salad for a stylish meal.

Serves 2
knob of butter
2 large field mushrooms, thinly sliced
2 garlic cloves, finely chopped
3 medium potatoes, peeled
150 ml (¼ pint) carton double cream
4 tablespoons milk
salt and freshly ground black pepper

1 Preheat the oven to 180C,350F, Gas 4. Heat the butter in a small pan and cook the mushrooms and garlic for 5 minutes until softened. Strain the liquid from the mushrooms into a jug.

2 Using a peeler, slice the potatoes into wafer-thin rounds, dropping them straight into a bowl of cold water. Drain the potatoes and pat dry with a clean tea towel.

3 Mix together the mushroom liquid, cream, milk and plenty of seasoning.

4 Layer the potatoes, mushrooms and cream in a greased ovenproof dish. Finish with a layer of potatoes and top with cream. Sprinkle over some freshly ground black pepper and bake in the oven for 1 hour until cooked through and crisp and golden on top.

SPICY POTATO HOTPOT

EASY!

**If you're short on time, this dish can be finished
on top of the stove rather than in the oven.**

Serves 2
2 tablespoons vegetable oil
1 small onion, finely chopped
1 small hot chilli, deseeded and finely chopped
2.5 cm (1 inch) piece fresh root ginger, finely chopped
2 garlic cloves, finely chopped
1 large potato, cubed
2 carrots, cubed
2 parsnips, cubed
1 teaspoon cornflour
450 ml (¾ pint) vegetable stock
*1 tablespoon Hot Chilli Sauce (page 145) or a few
drops Tabasco*
juice of a lime
seasoning

1 Preheat the oven to 200C, 400F, Gas 6. Heat the oil in a large pan and cook the onion, chilli, ginger and garlic for 2-3 minutes. Add the vegetable cubes and cook gently, stirring occasionally, for 10 minutes until they begin to brown.

2 Blend the cornflour with a little stock and add to the pan with the chilli sauce, lime juice and remaining stock. Bring to the boil, stirring until thickened, then season well to taste.

3 Transfer to a heatproof casserole dish and bake in the oven for 20 minutes until the vegetables are tender.

CLASSIC BAKED POTATO

REALLY EASY!

Baked potatoes make a great last-resort supper. A piping-hot stuffed potato is cheap, easy and nutritious, and the variety of fillings you can pile into a potato are endless. Choose an old main crop potato such as a King Edward rather than the new, thin skinned types. For a crunchy skin and floury, fluffy centre leave the potato in the oven for an extra 20 minutes, and for a softer skin, rub a little oil into the surface before cooking.

Serves 1

1 very large potato, weighing about 250g (8 oz)
small knob of butter
salt and freshly ground black pepper

1 Preheat the oven to 200C,400F, Gas 6. Scrub the potato in clean, cold water and pat dry.

2 Pierce the potato a few times with a fork. Place directly onto the oven shelf and bake for an hour until soft. Cut open and serve with butter and a sprinkle of salt and pepper.

GARLIC BUTTER POTATO

A plain baked potato smothered in garlic butter and served with a crisp green salad makes a simple, tasty supper.

Serves 1
1 hot baked potato, (see page 123)
30g (1 oz) butter
2 garlic cloves, crushed or finely chopped
1-2 tablespoons chopped fresh parsley
salt and freshly ground black pepper

1 Cut a large cross into the potato and squeeze the potato to open it out. Beat the butter with a wooden spoon to soften it then stir in the garlic, parsley, a little salt and plenty of black pepper. Spoon the mixture inside the potato and serve.

BAKED EGG AND CHEDDAR POTATO

Use the scooped out potato flesh for use in another dish such as Bubble and Squeak (Page 134) or Cheese and Chive Potato Cakes (page 130).

Serves 1
1 hot baked potato, (see page 123)
1 egg
30g (1 oz) Cheddar, grated
seasoning

1 Slice a lid about 2.5 cm (1 inch) thick off the top of the potato. Scoop out the flesh to leave a shell about 1 cm (½ inch) thick.

2 Season well inside the potato shell then crack the egg and place it carefully inside. Sprinkle over the cheese and replace the lid. Return to the oven for 10 minutes until the egg has set and the cheese has melted.

GARLIC BUTTER POTATO • BAKED EGG AND CHEDDAR POTATO

BAKED POTATO WITH MEXICAN TOPPING

This delicious combination can be used to fill pancakes or piled onto a lettuce-filled pitta.

Serves 1

1 hot baked potato, (see page 123)
4 tablespoons sour cream
1 small avocado, diced
2 tomatoes, skinned and diced
chilli seasoning

1 Cut the potato in half lengthwise and score deeply in a criss-cross pattern with a knife. Spoon over the sour cream and top with avocado and tomato dice. Sprinkle lightly with chilli seasoning and serve.

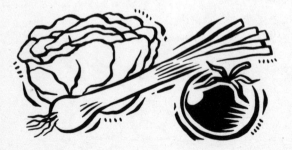

BAKED POTATO WITH YOGURT AND CRISPY ONOINS

Try using fromage frais or soft herb cheese in place of the yogurt.

Serves 1

1 hot baked potato, (see page 123)
1 teaspoon vegetable oil
1 small onion, sliced into rings
4-6 tablespoons Greek yogurt
1 tablespoon chopped fresh coriander or parsley
seasoning

1 Heat the oil in a small pan and fry the onions over a high heat for 5-7 minutes until crisp and golden brown. Remove and drain well.

2 Cut a large cross into the potato and squeeze the potato to open it out. Spoon in the Greek yogurt and top with onion, coriander and a little seasoning.

FETA AND OLIVE POTATO

**The tangy combination of feta cheese, olives
and lemon juice really gives the potato a lift.**

Serves 1
1 hot baked potato, (see page 123)
60g (2 oz) feta cheese, diced
1 tablespoon of pitted black olives, finely chopped
1 tablespoon olive oil
squeeze of lemon juice
seasoning

1 Cut a large cross into the potato and squeeze the
potato to open it out. Mix together the feta, chopped
olives, oil, lemon juice and seasoning. Spoon the
mixture inside the potato and serve.

LENTIL SHEPHERDS PIE

EASY!

**This hearty dish could feed up to 4 people if
served with other vegetables on the side,
however, on its own it is a complete meal for 2.
Keep any leftovers, covered, in the fridge and
reheat in the oven the following day.**

Serves 2

1 tablespoon vegetable oil
1 onion, finely chopped
1 carrot, finely diced
250g (8 oz) brown or green lentils
450 ml (¾ pint) vegetable stock
500g (1 lb) potatoes, peeled and cut into chunks
2 tablespoons milk
small knob of butter
seasoning
2 tomatoes, skinned and diced
60g (2 oz) frozen peas
1 tablespoon chopped fresh parsley or 1 teaspoon dried

1 Heat the oil in a large pan and fry the onion and carrot for 5 minutes until softened. Add the lentils and stock, cover and simmer for 30 minutes until tender.

2 Meanwhile, cook the potatoes in boiling salted water for 10-15 minutes until tender. Drain well and mash with milk, butter and seasoning.

3 Preheat the oven to 220C,425F, Gas 7. Stir the tomatoes, peas and parsley into the lentils and simmer together, uncovered, for 10 minutes. Season to taste and spoon into an ovenproof dish. Top with mashed potato and smooth down with the back of a fork. Bake in the oven for 15 minutes until golden brown and heated through.

FETA AND OLIVE POTATO • LENTIL SHEPHERDS PIE

129

CHEESE AND CHIVE POTATO CAKES

EASY!

The little pieces of cheese melt into the potato and add texture and flavour to these savoury cakes. Use whatever cheese you have in the fridge, mozzarella and Gruyère taste particularly good.

Serves 2
500g (1 lb) potatoes
60g (2 oz) soft cheese
60g (2 oz) Cheddar, finely diced
2 tablespoons chopped fresh chives
seasoning
2 tablespoons plain flour
1 egg, beaten
90g (3 oz) fresh breadcrumbs
vegetable oil for frying

1 Cook the potatoes in plenty of boiling salted water for 10-15 minutes until tender. Drain well, and mash together with the soft cheese. Stir in the diced Cheddar and chives and season to taste.

2 With floured hands, shape the mixture into 4 large, flat, even-sized cakes. Dust lightly with flour, then dip into the beaten egg and then the breadcrumbs.

3 Heat a little oil in a frying pan and gently cook the potato cakes for about 5 minutes on each side until crisp and golden. Remove from the pan with a palette knife and drain on kitchen paper.

SWEET POTATO STEW

REALLY EASY!

**All the vegetables in this stew are naturally
sweet-tasting so it makes a really warming,
sunny meal. If you can, use orange fleshed
sweet potatoes for this recipe, as they look
more attractive.**

Serves 2
2 tablespoons vegetable oil
500g (1 lb) sweet potatoes, scrubbed and cubed
1 large carrot, thickly sliced
250g (8 oz) can sweetcorn ,drained
300 ml (½ pint) vegetable stock
150g (5 oz) natural fromage frais
1 tablespoon chopped fresh parsley
seasoning

1 Heat the oil in a large saucepan and cook the sweet
potato and carrot for 10 minutes until beginning to
brown.

2 Stir in the sweetcorn and stock, bring to the boil and
simmer for 15 minutes until the vegetables are tender.
Add the fromage frais and parsley and season to taste.
Heat through and serve with crusty bread.

CHEESE AND CHIVE POTATO CAKES • SWEET POTATO STEW

WARM POTATO AND MUSHROOM SALAD

REALLY EASY!

This is a tasty way to use up leftover potatoes. In fact I much prefer them cooked this way to chips. Try serving on hot buttered toast.

Serves 1
2 cold, boiled potatoes,
2 tablespoons olive oil
seasoning
small knob of butter
1 garlic clove, finely chopped
125g (4 oz) button mushrooms
2 tablespoons water
2 tablespoons chopped fresh parsley or basil
1 tablespoon white wine vinegar
1 tablespoon freshly grated Parmesan

1 Cut the potatoes into cubes about the same size as the mushrooms. Toss the cubes with 1 tablespoon of oil and season well. Arrange on a baking sheet and place under a preheated grill for 15 minutes, turning occasionally until crisp and golden.

2 Meanwhile melt the butter in a small saucepan, add the garlic, mushrooms and 2 tablespoons of water, cover and cook gently for 15 minutes. Stir in the parsley and season to taste.

3 Place the potatoes in a bowl, add the mushrooms with their juices, the remaining oil and wine vinegar. Sprinkle over the Parmesan, toss well together and serve.

POTATO AND CARROT ROSTI

REALLY EASY!

This is the best ever Sunday brunch. It takes minutes to make and is really filling, but it is fried in oil so don't eat it every day.

Serves 1-2
2 medium potatoes
1 small carrot
seasoning
2 eggs
vegetable oil for frying

1 Peel the potatoes and carrot and grate coarsely into a bowl. Season with salt and pepper.

2 Heat a little oil in a frying pan, preferably non-stick. Tip the potatoes and carrot into the pan and flatten down with a fish slice. Cook over a fairly high heat until crisp and browned underneath. Turn over the rosti and cook for a further 3 minutes until browned on the second side.

3 Transfer to a warmed plate while you quickly fry the eggs in a little more oil. Top the rosti with the fried eggs and eat straightaway.

BUBBLE AND SQUEAK

REALLY EASY!

Use any sort of leafy green vegetable for this dish, Brussels sprouts and spinach both taste great.

Serves 1
1 large potato, cubed
knob of butter
2 large cabbage leaves, roughly chopped
2 tablespoons water
seasoning

1 Cook the potato in boiling salted water for 10-15 minutes until tender.

2 Meanwhile, heat the butter in a large frying pan, preferably non-stick, and stir-fry the cabbage with the water for about 7 minutes, until softened. Drain the potato well and add to the pan. Mash down roughly with a fork, then leave to cook for about 5 minutes until a crust forms on the bottom.

3 Break up the mixture and season to taste. Leave to cook for a further 5 minutes so that a crust again forms on the bottom. Slide onto a warm plate and serve with a dollop of tomato ketchup or a dash of Tabasco sauce.

GARLIC POTATO SOUP

REALLY EASY!

It is important that the garlic is crushed for this recipe – if you don't have a garlic crusher, sprinkle the peeled cloves with a little salt and flatten them under the blade of a heavy knife. If you only have Cheddar in the fridge, you can use it instead.

Serves 2

knob of butter or margarine
6 garlic cloves, crushed
500g (1 lb) potatoes, diced
600 ml (1 pint) vegetable stock
few drops Tabasco sauce
1 teaspoon white wine vinegar or lemon juice
1 tablespoon chopped fresh parsley
seasoning
60g (2 oz) feta or mozzarella cheese, thinly sliced

1 Heat the butter in a large saucepan and gently cook the garlic and potatoes for 5 minutes until beginning to turn golden. Add the stock, cover and simmer for 20 minutes until the potatoes are cooked and breaking up.

2 Use a masher to pound the potatoes into the soup – it's very hard to get it completely smooth, so don't worry. Stir in the Tabasco, vinegar and parsley and season to taste.

3 Ladle into bowls and sprinkle over the cheese. Serve immediately with hot buttered toast or warm crusty bread.

BUBBLE AND SQUEAK • GARLIC POTATO SOUP

POTATO AND CORN BAKE

REALLY EASY!

A creamy potato bake with cheese and sweetcorn.

Serves 2
500g (1 lb) potatoes, cubed
60g (2 oz) butter or margarine
125g (4 oz) Cheddar or other cheese, grated
150 ml (¼ pint milk)
3 eggs, beaten
180g (6 oz) drained canned sweetcorn (or use frozen
sweetcorn that has been thawed)
seasoning

1 Preheat the oven to 180C,350F, Gas 4. Cook the potatoes in plenty of boiling salted water for 10-15 minutes until tender. Drain well, and mash with the butter, cheese and little of the milk, until completely smooth. Beat in the remaining milk and the eggs.

2 Stir in the sweetcorn and season generously. Spoon into a greased heatproof dish and bake in the oven for 40 minutes, until set. Serve warm with Hot Chilli Sauce (page 45).

POTATO CURRY

REALLY EASY!

This tasty curry needs to be served with warm naan bread which can be bought ready-made from most supermarkets.

Serves 2
2 tablespoons vegetable oil
2 large potatoes, cut into 2.5 cm (1 inch) cubes
1 large onion, roughly chopped
1 tablespoon hot curry paste
7 tablespoons water
4 ripe tomatoes, skinned and quartered
4 garlic cloves, crushed
2 tablespoons chopped fresh coriander or parsley
Greek-style yogurt, to serve (optional)

1 Heat the oil in a large frying pan and add the potato, onions, curry paste and 2 tablespoons water. Cover and cook gently for 10-15 minutes, stirring occasionally, until the potato is tender and beginning to brown.

2 Stir in the tomatoes, garlic and about 5 tablespoons of water, cover and cook for a further 5 minutes until the tomatoes have softened but are still holding their shape. Sprinkle over the coriander and spoon onto plates. Drizzle over the yogurt, if using, and serve with naan bread.

POTATO AND CORN BAKE • POTATO CURRY

ITALIAN POTATO PIE

REALLY EASY!

For the perfect Sunday lunch, serve this melt-in-the-mouth pie with crisp green salad and a glass of Italian red wine.

Serves 2

500g (1 lb) potatoes, halved
4 tomatoes, skinned and thinly sliced
1 onion, finely chopped
1 teaspoon dried oregano
salt and freshly ground black pepper
150g (5 oz) mozzarella, sliced
4 tablespoons olive oil

1 Preheat the oven to 220C,425F, Gas 7.Cook the potatoes in plenty of boiling salted water for 15-20 minutes until tender. Drain well and slice thinly.

2 Arrange a layer of potatoes in a buttered, heatproof dish. Top with a layer of tomatoes sprinkled with onion, oregano and plenty of seasoning, and then a layer of mozzarella. Finish with a layer of potato topped with mozzarella.

3 Drizzle over the olive oil and bake in the oven for 20 minutes until crisp and golden brown.

POTATOES PROVENÇALE

REALLY EASY!

This French-style dish is easily adapted to make good use of any vegetables you have to hand – try adding canned cannellini beans or frozen peas.

Serves 2
2 tablespoons olive oil
2 large potatoes, diced
1 red pepper, deseeded and roughly chopped
1 onion, finely chopped
2 garlic cloves, finely chopped
200g (7 oz) can chopped tomatoes
30g (2 oz) black olives
2 tablespoons chopped fresh parsley or 1 teaspoon dried
salt and freshly ground black pepper

1 Heat the oil in a frying pan and stir-fry the diced potato and pepper for about 8 minutes until beginning to turn golden brown. Add the onion and garlic and continue to cook for a further 10-12 minutes until all the vegetables are tender and golden brown.

2 Add the tomatoes, olives, parsley and season to taste. Heat through for 2-3 minutes and serve with salad.

ITALIAN POTATO PIE • POTATOES PROVENÇALE

139

BRAISED SPINACH AND LEMONY MASH

REALLY EASY!

You could serve this spinach dish with pasta, rice or bread but it really does taste fantastic on a bed of smooth, lemon-flavoured mashed potatoes. You can use frozen spinach if you wish.

Serves 2
500g (1 lb) potatoes
juice of a lemon
knob of butter
seasoning
500g (1 lb) fresh spinach leaves
3 tablespoons olive oil
2 garlic cloves, thinly sliced
3 tomatoes, skinned and roughly chopped

1 Cook the potatoes in boiling salted water for 10-15 minutes until tender. Drain well and mash with the lemon juice, butter and seasoning until smooth and creamy.

2 Meanwhile, rinse the spinach leaves briefly in cold water and leave to drain in a colander. Heat the oil in large frying pan and when it is beginning to sizzle, throw in the garlic, tomatoes and damp spinach. Cover and simmer gently for 8 minutes until the spinach is soft and dark green.

3 Season the spinach to taste. Spoon the mashed potatoes onto plates, flattening down slightly, and pile the spinach mixture on top. Pour over any juices left in the pan and eat immediately.

SNACKS AND

STANDBYS

If you feel like a nibble, don't be tempted by crisps or chocolate. Dig deep into your cupboard and see if you can whip up a healthier, more filling snack to keep hunger at bay. However hard you might try, we all sometimes fancy a bite to eat between meals. It may be because you missed a meal and need something to keep you going or perhaps its just boredom, whatever the reason here are a few easy ideas to help you combat a snack attack.

WHITE BEAN PATÉ

REALLY EASY!

**This paté is delicious served on garlic toast.
Simply toast slices of French bread on both
sides, rub the top surface with a cut clove of
garlic and drizzle over a little olive oil. Keep
any paté that is left over covered, in the fridge
for 1-2 days.**

*3 tablespoons olive oil
3 garlic cloves, finely chopped
1 teaspoon chopped fresh rosemary (optional)
400g (14 oz) can cannellini or butter beans
salt and freshly ground black pepper*

1 Heat the olive oil in a saucepan, add the garlic and
rosemary and cook very gently for 5 minutes until the
garlic is lightly golden.

2 Drain the beans, reserving the liquid. Add the beans
to the pan with 2-3 tablespoons of the liquid and mash
down well with a fork to make a rough purée. Add
more liquid if needed and continue to cook for about 5
minutes until soft and creamy. Season to taste and eat
warm or cold.

HUMMUS

R E A L L Y   E A S Y !

**Tahini is sesame seed paste and can be bought
in health food shops and selected supermarkets.
If you prefer, you could use smooth peanut
butter in its place. Hummus will keep covered in
the fridge for a few days and is delicious spread
thickly on hot buttered toast.**

*400g (14 oz) can chick-peas, drained
2 garlic cloves, crushed
6 tablespoons olive oil
4 tablespoons tahini
½ teaspoon ground cumin
juice of a lemon
seasoning*

1 Mash together the chick-peas and garlic until fairly
smooth. Gradually beat in the olive oil to give a creamy
consistency.

2 Stir in the tahini, cumin, lemon juice and seasoning,
adding more, or less than the given amounts, to suit
your taste.

WHITE BEAN PATÉ • HUMMUS

MELTED
RED ONION TOASTS

REALLY EASY!

Try and buy red onions for this recipe as they are milder than ordinary onions and have a sweet flavour.

Serves 1
2 tablespoons olive oil
2 red onions, thinly sliced
1 garlic clove, thinly sliced
seasoning
1 thick slice of country bread
1 tablespoon mayonnaise
60g (2 oz) mozzarella or Cheddar, thinly sliced

1 Heat the oil in frying pan, add the onions and garlic cook very gently for 15 minutes until very soft and golden brown. Season well.

2 Toast the bread and spread with the mayonnaise. Pile on the onions, cover with the cheese and place under a preheated grill for 2-3 minutes until the cheese is bubbling. Eat immediately.

HOT CHILLI SAUCE

REALLY EASY!

This sauce in an essential standby. Stir it into pasta sauces, scrambled eggs, and serve on the side of countless plainer dishes for added flavour. If you have a liquidiser or a hand-held blender this sauce is incredibly quick to make, but the hand-chopped version, though a little rougher, is still very easy.

4 tomatoes
1 garlic clove, roughly chopped
1 onion roughly, chopped
2 hot red chillies, deseeded and roughly chopped
2 tablespoons chopped fresh parsley
1 tablespoon vegetable oil
seasoning

1 Push a fork into a tomato and hold in the flame of a gas ring for few seconds, turning until the skin blisters. Peel off the skin and discard. Repeat with the remaining tomatoes. If you do not have a gas cooker, place the tomatoes under a hot grill instead. Cut the tomatoes into quarters, scoop out and discard the seeds.

2 If you have a blender, whiz together the tomatoes, garlic, onion, chillies and parsley until smooth. If not, place them on a board and chop together with a heavy knife for as long as you can stand, until well-blended and fairly smooth.

3 Heat the vegetable oil in a frying pan, add the mixture and cook for about 10 minutes, stirring until thick and pulpy. Season well to taste and serve hot or cold.

MELTED RED ONION TOASTS • HOT CHILLI SAUCE

145

CHEESE PUFFS

REALLY EASY!

This snack is perfect for a midnight feast.

Serves 2
180g (6 oz) finely grated cheese
1 egg, beaten
1 teaspoon English mustard
seasoning
knob of butter or margarine
4 slices bread

1 Preheat the oven to 190C,375F, Gas 5. Mix together the cheese, egg, mustard and a little seasoning.

2 Butter the bread then spread thickly with the cheese mixture. Cut each slice into 4 triangles and place on a baking sheet. Cook in the oven for about 10 minutes until puffed and golden brown.

MASHED BANANA SANDWICH

REALLY EASY!

Serves 1
2 slices of bread
1 ripe banana
1 tablespoon clear honey

1 Toast the bread on both sides. Break the banana into 2 or 3 pieces and lay on top of the toast. Roughly mash into the toast with a fork then drizzle over the honey. Replace top slice of toast, cut in half and eat while still warm.

COURGETTE FRITTERS

EASY!

These little fritters are so delicious you may want to make double the quantity!

Serves 1-2
1 large courgette, grated
1 small onion, finely grated
1 small egg
4 tablespoons plain flour
½ teaspoon salt
vegetable oil for frying

1 Place the courgette and onion in a large bowl. Stir in the egg followed by the flour and salt.

2 Heat a little oil in a frying pan and drop in a heaped tablespoon of the mixture, spread out thinly with the back of the spoon and cook for 2-3 minutes on each side until crisp and golden. Drain on kitchen paper and serve with Hot Chilli Sauce (page 145).

CHEESE PUFFS • MASHED BANANA SANDWICH • COURGETTE FRITTERS

AUBERGINE APPETISER

EASY!

Serve this appetising paté with warm pitta bread and some strong black olives for a flavour-packed snack or starter. For a quick way to skin and deseed tomatoes, see Hot Chilli Sauce recipe on page 145.

Serves 2

1 large aubergine, halved
2 tablespoons olive oil
1 small onion, very finely chopped
2 garlic cloves, very finely chopped
2 ripe tomatoes, skinned, deseeded and very finely chopped
juice of half a lemon
2 tablespoons chopped fresh coriander or parsley
salt and freshly ground black pepper

1 Grill the aubergine for about 20 minutes, turning occasionally until the skin is soft and blackened.

2 Meanwhile, heat 1 tablespoon of the oil in a small frying pan and cook the onion and garlic for 5 minutes until softened.

3 Peel the skin from the aubergine and discard. Mash the flesh with a fork and stir in the onion mixture, remaining olive oil, tomatoes, lemon juice, coriander and plenty of seasoning.

NACHOS

REALLY EASY!

Try serving this Mexican snack with guacamole and sour cream for a light supper.

Serves 1
125g (4 oz) pack tortilla chips
200g (7 oz) can chopped tomatoes, drained
1 mild green chilli, deseeded and finely chopped
seasoning
60g (2 oz) Cheddar, grated

1 Empty the tortillas into a heatproof dish and pour over the chopped tomatoes. Sprinkle over the chilli and seasoning and place under a medium grill for 5-7 minutes until heated through.

2 Scatter the cheese over the top and return to the grill. Raise the heat and cook for a further 2-3 minutes until the cheese is bubbling. Eat immediately.

AUBERGINE APPETISER • NACHOS

FALAFEL

EASY!

**Give refectory food a miss and pack some
falafel in pitta pockets for your lunch. Or eat
with Greek salad for a satisfying supper.**

Serves 2-4
*400g (14 oz) can chick-peas, drained
half a small onion, very finely chopped
1 hot red chilli, very finely chopped
¼ teaspoon ground cumin
1 tablespoon chopped fresh coriander
1 egg, lightly beaten
2 tablespoons flour
vegetable oil for frying
seasoning*

1 Mash the chick-peas, onion, chilli, cumin and coriander well together and season to taste. It may take a while to get the mixture soft enough to shape, as chickpeas can be quite dry and firm, but persevere and the mixture should come together.

2 Shape into 8 round balls and flatten into patties. Dip first into the beaten egg and then into the flour, shaking off any excess. Heat the oil in a frying pan and cook the patties for 2-3 minutes until golden brown. Drain well on kitchen paper.

HASH BROWNS

REALLY EASY!

What do you eat if all you have in the house is a potato – and worse still, a cooked one? Simple, make a batch of crispy hash browns and serve with a dollop of brown sauce.

Serves 1
1-2 cold boiled potatoes
vegetable oil for frying
salt

1 Coarsely grate the potato into a bowl and sprinkle with salt. At this stage you may choose to add other flavourings such as onion or parsley.

2 Shape the mixture firmly into flat ovals. Heat 1 cm (½ inch) of oil in a small frying pan and cook the hash browns for 3-4 minutes on each side until crisp and golden.

3 Drain on kitchen paper and eat immediately. They can be reheated under a hot grill.

FALAFEL • HASH BROWNS

FRIED MOZZARELLA

EASY!

This snack is extra special if you use the mini balls of mozzarella that you can buy in supermarkets. Make sure the oil temperature is correct, if it is too hot, the breadcrumbs will brown too quickly before the cheese has melted in the centre. Likewise, if the oil is not hot enough, the cheese will melt and fall apart before the coating has become crisp and golden.

Serves 1
150g (5 oz) mozzarella
2 tablespoons plain flour
1 egg, beaten
seasoning
4 tablespoons fresh breadcrumbs
1 tablespoon chopped fresh parsley
vegetable oil for frying

1 Drain the mozzarella well on kitchen paper. Cut into bite-size pieces and toss in the flour.

2 Beat the egg with a little seasoning and mix the breadcrumbs with the parsley.

3 Dip the floured pieces into the beaten eggs and then the breadcrumbs. Make sure they are completely covered in crumbs.

4 Heat 4 cm (2 inch) of oil in a deep pan until a cube of bread turns golden in 1 minute. Fry the cheese bites for 1 minute until crisp and golden. Drain on kitchen paper and eat immediately.

REFRIED BEANS

REALLY EASY!

**Use these tasty beans as a filling for baked
potatoes, pancakes or pack into a ready-made
taco shell (which are readily available in
supermarkets), with some crisp lettuce
and a dollop of sour cream.**

Serves 2

knob of butter or 1 tablespoon of vegetable oil
1 onion, chopped
2 garlic cloves, finely chopped
200g (7 oz) can chopped tomatoes, drained
400g (14 oz) can kidney beans, drained
½ teaspoon chilli powder
salt

1 Heat the butter in a frying pan and gently cook the
onion and garlic for 5 minutes until softened. Add the
chopped tomatoes and heat through.

2 Add the beans a handful at a time, mashing them
down roughly with a fork.

3 Season with chilli powder and salt and heat through.

FRIED MOZZARELLA • REFRIED BEANS

APPLE AND BLUE CHEESE MUFFINS

REALLY EASY!

**Pan-fried apples and nuts with blue cheese
makes a great combination for any bread base.
Try with crumpets or toast.**

Serves 1

small knob of butter
1 dessert apple, sliced
1 tablespoon salted peanuts, roughly chopped
1 muffin, split open
30g (1 oz) blue cheese, e.g. Stilton, blue brie, dolcellate

1 Melt the butter in a small frying pan and when sizzling toss in the apples and nuts. Cook over a fairly high heat for 4-5 minutes until golden.

2 Spoon onto the open muffin halves and crumble over the cheese. Pop under a preheated grill for 2-3 minutes until bubbling. Eat at once!

FRIED MUSHROOMS

REALLY EASY!

These mushrooms make a delicious snack if served on a thick slice of buttered toast. Top with a fried egg for an even tastier and more substantial snack.

Serves 1
small knob of butter
½ an onion, finely chopped
125g (4 oz) mushrooms, sliced
1 tablespoon freshly grated Parmesan
seasoning
thick slice of hot buttered toast, to serve

1 Heat the butter in a small frying pan and gently cook the onion and mushrooms for 5 minutes until golden. Stir in the Parmesan and season to taste. Tip the mixture onto the hot toast and eat.

TOMATO AND BREAD

REALLY EASY!

This is a classic peasant snack from southern Italy. The field workers and farmers take a chunk of bread, handful of tomatoes and flask of olive oil out with them and assemble it for their lunch. My mother often gave me this as a snack after school and it's still a favourite standby of mine.

Serves 1

1 ripe tomato
Thick slice of bread, e.g. ciabatta or rustic-style country bread or use the crust from a sliced white loaf
2 fresh basil leaves (optional)
extra virgin olive oil
coarse salt

1 Cut the tomato in half and place the halves cut side down on the bread. Squash the tomatoes into the bread so that the juices and seeds soak in and the flesh breaks up a little. Roughly tear the basil leaves, if using, and scatter them on top. Drizzle over about a tablespoon of olive oil and sprinkle with salt.

SCOTCH PANCAKES

E A S Y !

Turn these brilliant Scotch pancakes into American ones by skipping the sultanas and lemon and adding a handful of fresh blueberries or raspberries and drizzling them with maple syrup before serving.

Serves 2-4
250g (8 oz) self raising flour
1 teaspoon baking powder
30g (1 oz) sugar
pinch of salt
2 eggs, beaten
300 ml (½ pint) milk
45g (1½ oz) butter or margarine, melted
30g (1 oz) sultanas
grated rind of ½ a lemon (optional)
oil for frying

1 Sieve the flour, baking powder, sugar and salt into a bowl. Add the eggs and half the milk and beat with a wooden spoon until smooth.

2 Beat in the remaining milk and the melted butter to give a thick batter. Stir in the sultanas and lemon rind, if using, and leave to rest for about 5 minutes.

3 Heat a little oil in a large frying pan and drop in large spoonfuls of batter . Cook for a couple of minutes until bubbles rise to the surface and the pancakes are golden underneath. Flip over and cook the other side. Drain on kitchen paper and serve in a stack.

TOMATO AND BREAD • SCOTCH PANCAKES

157

PIPERADE

REALLY EASY!

**This a classic French dish which is a cross
between an omelette and scrambled eggs, with
a savoury filling.**

Serves 2
1 tablespoon olive oil
1 red onion, sliced
1 garlic clove, finely chopped
1 large red pepper, deseeded and sliced
4 eggs
4 tablespoons milk
2 tablespoons chopped fresh parsley
seasoning

1 Heat the oil in a large frying pan and gently cook the onion, garlic and pepper for about 8 minutes until softened.

2 Beat together the eggs, milk, parsley and seasoning and add to the pan.

3 Scramble together for 2 minutes until the eggs are just cooked. Serve with salad, a baked potato or on hot buttered toast for a quick snack or light lunch.

INDEX